AWS CodeStar User Guide

A catalogue record for this book is available from the Hong Kong Public Libraries.

Published in Hong Kong by Samurai Media Limited.

Email: info@samuraimedia.org

ISBN 9789888408597

Contents

What Is AWS CodeStar?

AWS CodeStar is a cloud-based service for creating, managing, and working with software development projects on AWS. You can quickly develop, build, and deploy applications on AWS with an AWS CodeStar project. An AWS CodeStar project creates and integrates AWS services for your project development toolchain. Depending on your choice of AWS CodeStar project template, that toolchain might include source control, build, deployment, virtual servers or serverless resources, and more. AWS CodeStar also manages the permissions required for project users (called team members). By adding users as team members to an AWS CodeStar project, project owners can quickly and simply grant each team member role-appropriate access to a project and its resources.

The following video provides a brief introduction to AWS CodeStar.

Topics

- What Can I Do with AWS CodeStar?
- A Quick Look at AWS CodeStar
- How Do I Get Started with AWS CodeStar?

What Can I Do with AWS CodeStar?

You can use AWS CodeStar to help you set up your application development in the cloud and manage your development from a single, centralized dashboard. Specifically, you can:

- **Start new software projects on AWS in minutes using templates for web applications, web services and more:** AWS CodeStar includes AWS CodeStar project templates for various project types and programming languages. Because AWS CodeStar takes care of the setup, all your project resources are configured to work together.
- **Manage project access for your team**: AWS CodeStar provides a central console where you can assign project team members the roles they need to access tools and resources. These permissions are applied automatically across all AWS services used in your project, so you don't need to create or manage complex IAM policies.
- **Visualize, operate, and collaborate on your projects in one place**: AWS CodeStar includes a project dashboard that provides an overall view of the project, its toolchain, and important events. You can monitor the latest project activity, like recent code commits, and track the status of your code changes, build results, and deployments, all from the same web page. You can monitor what's going on in the project from a single dashboard and drill into problems to investigate.
- **Iterate quickly with all the tools you need**: AWS CodeStar includes an integrated development toolchain for your project. Team members push code, and changes are automatically deployed. Integration with issue tracking allows team members to keep track of what needs to be done next. You and your team can work together more quickly and efficiently across all phases of code delivery.

A Quick Look at AWS CodeStar

The following shows an example dashboard for a software project in AWS CodeStar.

In this example, a project pipeline in AWS CodePipeline ensures that each code push made to an AWS CodeCommit repository is built and deployed to an Amazon EC2 instance using AWS CodeDeploy. The most recent commit messages, deployment statistics, and deployment status are displayed. You can drill down on the specifics of any commits, builds, or deployments.

How Do I Get Started with AWS CodeStar?

To get started with AWS CodeStar:

1. **Prepare** to use AWS CodeStar by following the steps in Setting Up AWS CodeStar.

2. **Experiment** with AWS CodeStar by following the steps in the Getting Started with AWS CodeStar walkthrough.

3. **Share** your project with other developers by following the steps in Add Team Members to an AWS CodeStar Project .

4. **Expand** your AWS CodeStar project by adding integration with your favorite IDE by following the steps in Use an IDE with AWS CodeStar.

Setting Up AWS CodeStar

Before you can start using AWS CodeStar, you must complete the following steps. The account you use to sign in to AWS must be configured to allow the following actions:

Topics

- Step 1: Create an AWS Account
- Step 2: Create the AWS CodeStar Service Role
- Step 3: Configure the User's IAM Permissions
- Step 4: Create an Amazon EC2 Key Pair for AWS CodeStar Projects
- Step 5: Open the AWS CodeStar Console
- Next Steps

Step 1: Create an AWS Account

Create an AWS account by going to https://aws.amazon.com/ and choosing **Sign Up**.

Step 2: Create the AWS CodeStar Service Role

AWS CodeStar requires the creation of a service role in order to create and manage AWS resources and IAM permissions. You only need to create the service role once.

Important
You must be signed in as an IAM administrative user (or root account) in order to create this service role. For more information about administrative users, see Creating Your First IAM User and Group.

1. Open the AWS CodeStar console at https://console.aws.amazon.com/codestar/.

2. Choose **Start project**. (If you do not see **Start project** but instead are directed to the projects list page, the service role has been created. You can jump ahead to Configure Permissions for IAM Users.)

3. In **Create service role**, choose **Yes, create role**.

4. Exit the wizard. You'll come back to this later.

Step 3: Configure the User's IAM Permissions

You can use AWS CodeStar as an IAM user, a federated user, the root user, or an assumed role. If you choose an IAM user, AWS CodeStar helps you configure user access by managing IAM permissions for you. For a summary of what AWS CodeStar can do for IAM users versus federated users, see AWS CodeStar Access Permissions Reference.

Configure Permissions for IAM Users

Complete these steps to set up IAM user permissions.

1. To perform this step, you must have signed in to the console either as a root user, an IAM administrator user in the account, or an IAM user or federated user with the associated AdministratorAccess managed policy or equivalent. Attach the **AWSCodeStarFullAccess** managed policy to the IAM user who will create the project. This policy allows you to create an AWS CodeStar project.

2. Sign in as the user who will create the project, and then create your project as described in Step 1: Create an AWS CodeStar Project. AWS CodeStar creates the Owner, Contributor, and Viewer managed policies for the project. As the project creator, your project Owner permissions are applied automatically.

3. After you have created your project, use your permissions to add other IAM users as team members to your project. See Manage Permissions for AWS CodeStar Team Members .

4. If your IAM user has already been added to one or more AWS CodeStar projects, it already has the policies and permissions required to access the service and resources for the projects you belong to. To set up your local computer for working with AWS CodeStar projects, follow the steps in Getting Started. You can also sign in to the AWS CodeStar console and configure your user profile. For more information, see Manage Display Information for Your AWS CodeStar User Profile and Add a Public Key to Your AWS CodeStar User Profile .

If you have not set up any IAM users, see IAM user for information about setting up an IAM user.

Configure Permissions for Federated Users

To use AWS CodeStar as a federated user, the federated user needs IAM permissions that allow them to use AWS CodeStar APIs and access any resources used in the projects (such as Amazon EC2 or AWS Lambda). The following steps show how to configure these permissions.

1. To perform this step, you must have signed in to the console either as a root user, an IAM administrator user in the account, or an IAM user or federated user with the associated AdministratorAccess managed policy or equivalent. Attach the **AWSCodeStarFullAccess** managed policy to the federated user role that will create the project. See Attach the `AWSCodeStarFullAccess` Managed Policy to the Federated User's Role.

2. Sign in the with role that will create the project, and then create your project as described in Step 1: Create an AWS CodeStar Project. AWS CodeStar creates the Owner, Contributor, and Viewer managed policies for the project. As the federated user project creator, your project Owner permissions are not applied automatically. You might not be able to access all project resources. Perform the next step to configure your Owner permissions and give yourself access all project resources.

3. To perform this step, you must have signed in to the console either as a root user, an IAM administrator user in the account, or an IAM user or federated user with the associated AdministratorAccess managed policy or equivalent. Attach your project's AWS CodeStar Owner managed policy to the role you assume as a federated user. This allows you to manage and view all of the resources created for your project. See Attach Your Project's AWS CodeStar Viewer/Contributor/Owner Managed Policy to the Federated User's Role.

4. To perform this step, you must have signed in to the console either as a root user, an IAM administrator user in the account, or an IAM user or federated user with the associated AdministratorAccess managed policy or equivalent. Grant federated users access to your project by attaching the appropriate AWS CodeStar Owner/Contributor/Viewer managed policy to the user's role. See Attach Your Project's AWS CodeStar Viewer/Contributor/Owner Managed Policy to the Federated User's Role.

If you have not set up any federated users, see Federated User Access to AWS CodeStar.

Step 4: Create an Amazon EC2 Key Pair for AWS CodeStar Projects

Many AWS CodeStar projects use AWS CodeDeploy or AWS Elastic Beanstalk to deploy code to Amazon Elastic Compute Cloud (Amazon EC2) instances. To access Amazon EC2 instances associated with your project, create an Amazon EC2 key pair for your IAM user. Your IAM user must have permissions to create and manage Amazon EC2 keys (for example, permission to take the actions `ec2:CreateKeyPair` and `ec2:ImportKeyPair`). For more information, see Amazon EC2 Key Pairs.

Step 5: Open the AWS CodeStar Console

Sign in to the AWS Management Console, and then open the AWS CodeStar console at https://console.aws.amazon.com/codestar/.

Next Steps

Congratulations, you have completed the setup! To start working with AWS CodeStar, see Getting Started with AWS CodeStar.

Getting Started with AWS CodeStar

In this walkthrough, you'll use AWS CodeStar to create a web application. This project includes sample code in a source repository, a continuous deployment toolchain, and a project dashboard where you can view and monitor your project.

By following the steps, you will:

- Create a project in AWS CodeStar.
- Explore the project.
- Commit a code change.
- See your code change deployed automatically.
- Add other people to work on your project.
- Clean up project resources when they're no longer needed.

Note

If you haven't already, complete the steps in Setting Up AWS CodeStar before you start this walkthrough, including Step 2: Create the AWS CodeStar Service Role while logged in with an account that is an administrative user in IAM. To create a project, you must sign in to the AWS Management Console using an IAM user that has the **AWSCodeStarFullAccess** policy.

Topics

- Step 1: Create an AWS CodeStar Project
- Step 2: Add Display Information for Your AWS CodeStar User Profile
- Step 3: View Your Project
- Step 4: Customize the Team Wiki Tile and the Project Dashboard
- Step 5: Commit a Change
- Step 6: Add More Team Members
- Step 7: Clean Up
- Step 8: Ready Your Project for a Production Environment
- Next Steps
- Tutorial: Creating and Managing a Serverless Project in AWS CodeStar

Step 1: Create an AWS CodeStar Project

In this step, you'll create a JavaScript (Node.js) software development project for a web application. You'll use an AWS CodeStar project template to create the project.

Note

This walkthrough uses an AWS CodeStar project template with the following options:
Application category: Web application **Programming language**: Node.js **AWS Service**: Amazon EC2 If you choose other options, your experience might not match what's documented in this walkthrough.

To create a project in AWS CodeStar

1. Sign in to the AWS Management Console, and then open the AWS CodeStar console at https://console.
aws.amazon.com/codestar/.

   Make sure that you are signed in to the AWS region where you want to create the project and its resources. For example, to create a project in US East (Ohio), make sure you have that region selected. For information about AWS regions where AWS CodeStar is available, see Regions and Endpoints in the *AWS General Reference* .

2. On the **AWS CodeStar** page, choose **Create a new project**. (If you are the first user to create a project, choose **Start a project**.)

3. On the **Choose a project template** page, choose the project type from the list of AWS CodeStar project templates. You can use the filter bar to narrow your choices. For example, for a web application project written in Node.js that will be deployed to Amazon EC2 instances, select the **Web application**, **Node.js**, and **Amazon EC2** check boxes. Then choose from the templates available for that set of options.

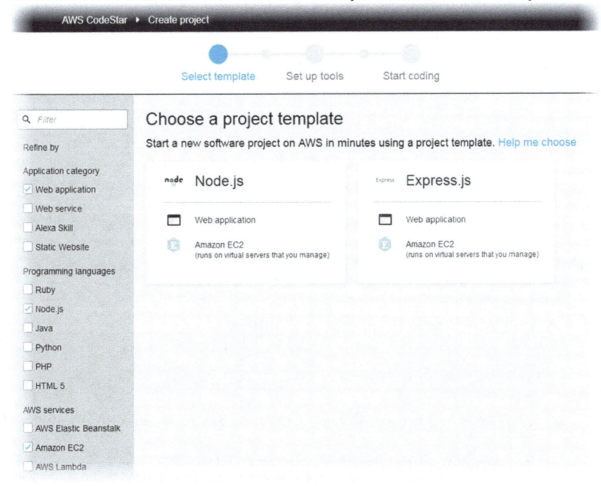

For more information, see AWS CodeStar Project Templates.

4. In **Project name**, type a name for the project, such as *My First Project*. The ID for the project is derived from this project name, but is limited to 15 characters.

For example, the default ID for a project named *My First Project* is *my-first-projec*. This project ID is the basis for the names of all resources associated with the project. For example, AWS CodeStar uses this project ID as part of the URL for your code repository as well as the names of related security access roles and policies in IAM. After the project is created, the project ID cannot be changed, so make sure you are okay with this project ID. To edit the project ID before you create the project, choose **Edit**.

For information about the limits on project names and project IDs, see Limits in AWS CodeStar. **Note** Project IDs must be unique for your AWS account within an AWS region.

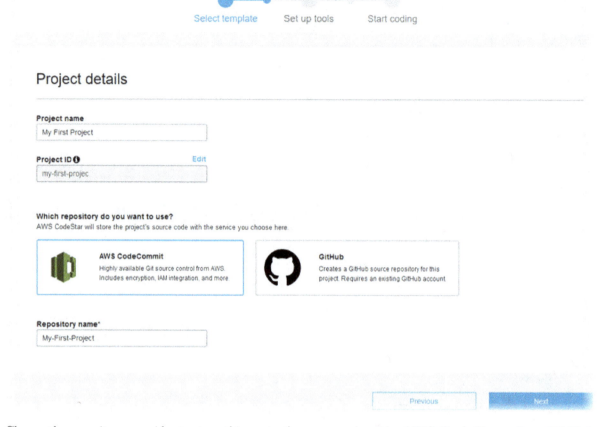

5. Choose the repository provider to store this project's source code with: **AWS CodeCommit** or **GitHub**.

6. If you chose **AWS CodeCommit**, for **Repository name**, accept the default AWS CodeCommit repository name that AWS CodeStar suggests, or type a different AWS CodeCommit repository name of your choice. Then skip ahead to step 8 in this procedure.

7. If you chose **GitHub**, then choose **Connect with GitHub**.

   1. If the **Sign in to GitHub** page is displayed, type your GitHub username or email address and password, and then choose **Sign in**. **Note** To complete this page, you must have a GitHub account. For more information, see Join GitHub on the GitHub website.

   2. If the **Two-factor authentication** page displays, for **Authentication code**, type the code that GitHub sends you. Then choose **Verify**.

   3. On the **Authorize AWS CodeStar** page, choose **Authorize**. **Note** When you choose **Authorize**, you allow AWS CodeStar to create a GitHub repository for your personal GitHub account, or for any GitHub organization where you have permissions (which is marked with a green check icon in **Organization access**).
To add a GitHub organization to the **Organization access** list, ask one of the organization's owners to invite you to the organization by following the instructions in Inviting users to join your organization on the GitHub Help website. After you join the organization, refresh the **Authorize AWS CodeStar** page to see the organization in the list.
To get permissions to authorize a GitHub organization that is in the list but does not have a green check icon, choose **Grant**. If you see **Request** instead, choose it, and then ask one of the organization's owners to allow AWS CodeStar to create a GitHub repository in the organization by following the

instructions in Approving OAuth Apps for your organization on the GitHub Help website. After the owner does this, refresh the **Authorize AWS CodeStar** page to see the **Grant** button.

4. For **Owner**, choose the GitHub organization or your personal GitHub account that you want AWS CodeStar to create the GitHub repository for.

5. For **Repository name**, accept the default GitHub repository name that AWS CodeStar suggests, or type a different GitHub repository name of your choice.

6. Choose **Public repository** or **Private repository** to make the GitHub repository public or private.
Note
Depending on your GitHub account type, GitHub may not allow you to create a private repository. For more information, see GitHub Pricing on the GitHub website.

7. For **Repository description**, provide an optional description for the GitHub repository.

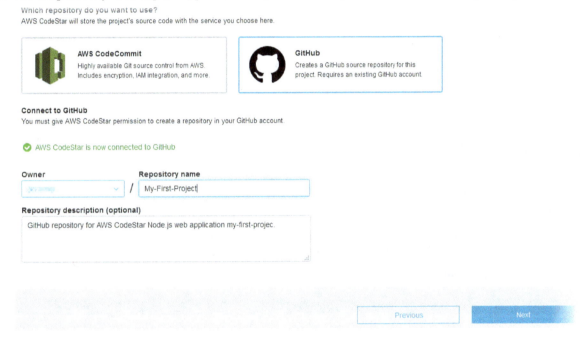

8. Choose **Next**.

9. Review the resources and configuration details. Choose **Edit Amazon EC2 Configuration** (where available) if your project will deploy to Amazon EC2 instances and you want to make changes. For example, you can choose from available instance types for your project. **Note**
Different Amazon EC2 instance types provide different levels of computing power and might have different associated costs. For more information, see Amazon EC2 Instance Types and Amazon EC2 Pricing.
If you have more than one virtual private cloud (VPC) or multiple subnets created in Amazon Virtual Private Cloud, you can also choose the VPC and subnet to use. However, if you choose an Amazon EC2 instance type that is not supported on dedicated instances, you cannot choose a VPC whose instance tenancy is set to **Dedicated**.
For more information, see What Is Amazon VPC? and Dedicated Instance Basics.

10. Leave the **AWS CodeStar would like permission to administer AWS resources on your behalf** check box selected. If this box is not selected, you will not be able to create a project. For more information about the service role, the policy, and its permissions, see AWS CodeStar Service Role Policy and Permissions.

Choose **Next** or **Create project**. (The displayed choice depends on your project template.)

11. In **Choose an Amazon EC2 Key Pair**, choose the Amazon EC2 key pair you created in Step 4: Create an Amazon EC2 Key Pair for AWS CodeStar Projects in *Setting Up*. Select **I acknowledge that I have**

access to the private key file for this key pair, and then choose **Create project**.

12. It might take a few minutes to create the project (including the repository). After your project has a repository, you can use the **Set up tools** page to configure access to it, or you can choose **Skip** and configure access later. After your project has been created, you will see a **Welcome** tile that contains useful links. You can use these links to optionally configure other items, such as your user profile in AWS CodeStar.

Step 2: Add Display Information for Your AWS CodeStar User Profile

When you create a project, you're added to the project team as an owner. If this is the first time you've used AWS CodeStar, you'll be asked to provide additional information, such as:

- Your display name to show to other users.
- The email address to show to other users.

This information is used in your AWS CodeStar user profile. User profiles are not project-specific, but are limited to an AWS region. If you belong to projects in more than one region, you'll have to create a user profile in each region. Each regional profile can contain different information, if you prefer.

Provide a user name and email address when prompted, and then choose **Next**.

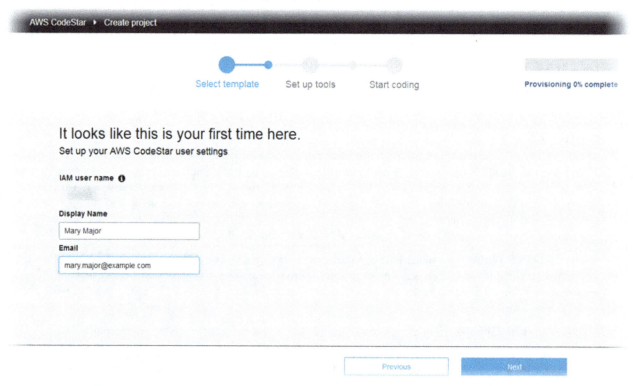

Note

This user name and email address is used in your AWS CodeStar user profile. If your project uses resources outside of AWS, for example a GitHub repository or issues in Atlassian JIRA, those resource providers may use separate user profiles, which may have different user names and email addresses. For more information, see the resource provider's documentation.

Step 3: View Your Project

Your AWS CodeStar project dashboard is where you and your team view the status of your project resources, including the latest commits to your project, the state of your continuous delivery pipeline, and the performance of your instances. This information is displayed on tiles that are dedicated to a particular resource. To see more information about any of these resources, choose the details link on the tile. The console for that AWS service will open on the details page for that resource.

You can change where each tile appears on your dashboard by dragging and dropping it to a new location. You can also use the ellipsis menu on each tile to remove that tile from the display. To add a tile, choose **Add tile** in the dashboard, and choose any tile that is not already present.

In your new project, you'll see the following tiles:

- The **Welcome** tile contains links to actions you might want to perform. Unlike other tiles, you cannot move this tile to another location, or add it back after closing it.

- The **Continuous deployment** tile displays a summary view of the continuous delivery pipeline for your project. The pipeline deploys the web application code when there is a change in your repository. Because your project is new, the pipeline immediately starts deploying the sample code. You can see the processing and completion of each stage as your web application is deployed. For a deployment stage, choose **Endpoint** to view a link to that endpoint (if you chose the project template suggested at the start of this walkthrough, it's an Amazon EC2 instance where your sample web application is deployed and running).

  You can also see if a stage has a problem or requires approval. To see details about the state of the pipeline, its stages, and its actions, or to make changes such as adding or editing a stage, choose **AWS CodePipeline details**.

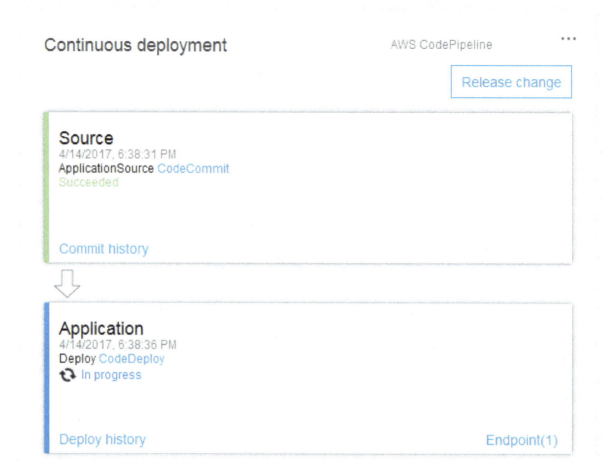

- The **Application endpoints** tile displays links to the endpoints where you can view your software. This is the same link you saw in the **Continuous deployment** tile. Choose the link to view your application or service.

- The **Commit history** tile displays the recent commit history of the repository. When you first create a project, the most recent commit is the one made by AWS CodeStar. This commit started running the sample code through the pipeline. When you make another commit, that will appear in the history, too. That code change will start running through the pipeline automatically. To view the commits of a different branch, use the branch selector button. To view all commits or other details about the commits or the repository, choose **AWS CodeCommit details** (if the code is stored in AWS CodeCommit) or **Open in GitHub** (if the source code is stored in GitHub).

- The **Application activity** tile displays Amazon CloudWatch metrics for your project. For example, it displays the CPU utilization of any Amazon EC2 instances deployed to by AWS Elastic Beanstalk or AWS CodeDeploy resources in your pipeline. In projects that use AWS Lambda, it displays invocation and error metrics for the Lambda function. This information is displayed by the hour. If you used the suggested AWS CodeStar project template for this walkthrough, you should see a noticeable spike in activity as your application is first deployed to those instances. You can refresh monitoring to see changes in your instance health, which can help you identify problems or the need for more resources.

Note

If your AWS CodeStar project includes more than one metric, you can filter the display by choosing a particular metric in the tile.

- The **JIRA** tile is for integrating your AWS CodeStar project with an existing Atlassian JIRA project. Configuring this tile will enable you and your project team to track JIRA issues from the project dashboard. To configure this tile, choose **Connect** and follow the instructions.

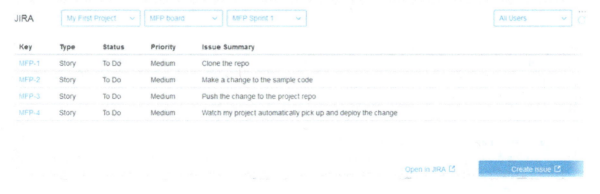

- There is also a **Team wiki tile**. You can customize the contents of this tile to store team notes, link to useful resources for your team project, provide samples, and so on. You'll customize this tile in the next step.

Step 4: Customize the Team Wiki Tile and the Project Dashboard

Each AWS CodeStar project includes a customizable team wiki tile that can be used for any purpose (for example, adding links to team resources or showing code snippets for a preferred development style). This tile supports both plain text and formatted content. In this step, you'll customize this tile to include a link to the AWS DevOps blog.

To customize the team wiki tile

1. In the project dashboard, on the team wiki tile, choose the ellipsis menu, and then choose **Edit**.

2. In **Widget title**, type *Team links*. In **Markdown content**, add an item to the list and paste the following:

```
1 [AWS DevOps Blog](https://aws.amazon.com/blogs/devops/)
```

Choose **Save**.

3. Choose the link on the tile to test it.

To customize your dashboard appearance

1. Choose one of the tiles on the dashboard. Drag and drop it to a new position. You can rearrange dashboard tiles to help ensure the information most important to you is in the most visible positions.

2. To remove a tile, choose the ellipsis menu (**...**) on that tile, and then choose **Remove from Dashboard**.

3. To add a tile, choose **Add tile** at the top of the dashboard, and then choose the tile to add. You can only have one of each kind of tile on your dashboard.

Step 5: Commit a Change

First, take a look at the sample code that was included in your project, and see what the application looks like. On the **Application endpoints** tile, choose the link to your endpoint. Your sample web application is displayed in a new window or browser tab. This is the project sample that AWS CodeStar built and deployed.

If you'd like to look at the code itself, in the navigation bar, choose **Code**. Your project's repository opens in a new tab or window. Read the contents of the repository's readme file (**README.md**), and browse the content of those files.

In this step, you will make a change to the code and then push that change to your repository. You can do this in one of several ways:

- If the project's code is stored in an AWS CodeCommit or GitHub repository, you can use AWS Cloud9 to work with the code directly from your web browser, without installing any additional tools. For more information, see Create an AWS Cloud9 Environment for a Project.
- If the project's code is stored in an AWS CodeCommit repository, and you have Visual Studio or Eclipse installed, you can use the AWS Toolkit for Visual Studio or AWS Toolkit for Eclipse to more easily connect to the code. For more information, see Use an IDE with AWS CodeStar. If you don't have Visual Studio or Eclipse installed, then install a Git client, and follow the instructions later in this step.
- If the project's code is stored in a GitHub repository, you can use your IDE's tools for connecting to GitHub. For example:
  - For Visual Studio, you can use a tools such as the GitHub Extension for Visual Studio. For more information, see the Overview page on the GitHub Extension for Visual Studio website and Getting Started with GitHub for Visual Studio on the GitHub website.

- For Eclipse, you can use a tool such as EGit for Eclipse. For more information, see the EGit website and EGit Documentation on the EGit website.
- For other IDEs, consult your IDE's documentation.
- For other types of code repositories, see the repository provider's documentation.

The following instructions show how to make a basic change to the sample.

To set up your computer to commit changes (IAM User) Note

This procedure assumes that your project's code is stored in an AWS CodeCommit repository. For other types of code repositories, see the repository provider's documentation, and then skip ahead to the next procedure, "To clone the project repository and make a change."

If the code is stored in AWS CodeCommit, and you are already using AWS CodeCommit or you used the AWS CodeStar console to create an AWS Cloud9 development environment for the project, you don't need more configuration. Skip ahead to the next procedure, "To clone the project repository and make a change."

1. Install Git on your local computer.

2. Sign in to the AWS Management Console and open the IAM console at https://console.aws.amazon.com/iam/.

   Sign in as the IAM user who will use Git credentials for connections to your AWS CodeStar project repository in AWS CodeCommit.

3. In the IAM console, in the navigation pane, choose **Users**, and from the list of users, choose your IAM user.

4. On the user details page, choose the **Security Credentials** tab, and in **HTTPS Git credentials for AWS CodeCommit**, choose **Generate**.

Note
You cannot choose your own user name or password for Git credentials. For more information, see Use Git Credentials and HTTPS with AWS CodeCommit.

5. Copy the user name and password that IAM generated for you. You can choose **Show** and then copy and paste this information into a secure file on your local computer, or you can choose **Download credentials** to download this information as a .CSV file. You will need this information to connect to AWS CodeCommit.

Git credentials generated

IAM has generated a user name and password for you to use when authenticating to AWS CodeCommit. You can use these credentials when connecting to AWS CodeCommit from your local computer and from tools that require a static user name and password. Learn more

User name   MyDemoUser-

Password   ••••••••• Show

This is the only time the password will be available to view, copy, or download. We recommend downloading these credentials and storing the file in a secure location. You can reset the password in IAM at any time.

Download credentials   Close

After you have saved your credentials, choose **Close**. **Important**
This is your only chance to save the user name and password. If you do not save them, you can copy the user name from the IAM console, but you cannot look up the password. You must reset the password and then save it.

To set up your computer to commit changes (Federated User)

You can use the console to upload files to your repository, or you can connect from your local computer using Git. If you are using federated access, follow these steps to connect to and clone your repository from your local computer using Git. **Note**
This procedure assumes that your project's code is stored in an AWS CodeCommit repository. For other types of code repositories, see the repository provider's documentation, and then skip ahead to the next procedure, "To clone the project repository and make a change."

1. Install Git on your local computer.

2. Install the AWS CLI.

3. Configure your temporary security credentials for a federated user. To learn how to do this, see Temporary Access to AWS CodeCommit Repositories. For more information about temporary credentials, see Permissions for GetFederationToken. Temporary credentials consist of the following:

   - AWS access key
   - AWS secret key
   - Session token

4. Connect to your repository using the AWS CLI credential helper. For information, see Setup Steps for HTTPS Connections to AWS CodeCommit Repositories on Linux, macOS, or Unix with the AWS CLI Credential Helper or Setup Steps for HTTPS Connections to AWS CodeCommit Repositories on Windows with the AWS CLI Credential Helper

5. The following example provides the steps to connect to an AWS CodeCommit repository and push a commit to it.

Example: To clone the project repository and make a change Note

This procedure shows how to clone the project's code repository to your computer, make a change to the project's `index.html` file, and then push your change to the remote repository. This procedure assumes that your project's code is stored in an AWS CodeCommit repository and that you're using a Git client from the command line. For other types of code repositories or tools, see the provider's documentation for how to clone the repository, change the file, and then push the code.

1. If you used the AWS CodeStar console to create an AWS Cloud9 development environment for the project, open the development environment, and then skip ahead to step 3 in this procedure. To open the development environment, see Open an AWS Cloud9 Environment for a Project.

   With your project open in the AWS CodeStar console, on the navigation bar, choose the **Project** gear icon, and then choose the **Connect tools** button. In the drop-down list next to **Clone repository URL**, choose the protocol for the connection type you have set up for AWS CodeCommit, and then copy the link. For example, if you followed the steps in the previous procedure to set up Git credentials for AWS CodeCommit, choose **HTTPS**.

2. On your local computer, open a terminal or command line window and change directories to a temporary directory. Run the git clone command to clone the repository to your computer. Paste the link you copied. For example, for AWS CodeCommit using HTTPS:

   ```
   1 git clone https://git-codecommit.us-east-2.amazonaws.com/v1/repos/my-first-projec
   ```

   The first time you connect, you will be prompted for the user name and password for the repository. For AWS CodeCommit, type the Git credentials user name and password you downloaded in the previous procedure.

3. Navigate to the clone directory on your computer and browse the contents.

4. Open the `index.html` file in an editor and make a change to the file. For example, you could change the header text from `<H1>Congratulations!</H1>` to the following:

   ```
   1 <H1>I did it!</H1>
   ```

   Save the file.

5. At the terminal or command prompt, add your changed file, and then commit and push your change:

   ```
   1 git add index.html
   2 git commit -m "Making my first change to the web app"
   3 git push
   ```

6. On your project dashboard, view the changes in progress. You'll see that the commit history for the repository is updated with your commit, including the commit message. You can also see the pipeline pick up your change to the repository and start building and deploying it. You can use the links you added to the project information tile to view your change to the web application after it is deployed. **Note** If **Failed** is displayed for any of the pipeline stages, see the following for troubleshooting help:
   For the **Source** stage, see Troubleshooting AWS CodeCommit in the *AWS CodeCommit User Guide*. For the **Build** stage, see Troubleshooting AWS CodeBuild in the *AWS CodeBuild User Guide*. For the **Deploy** stage, see Troubleshooting AWS CloudFormation in the *AWS CloudFormation User Guide*. For other issues, see Troubleshooting AWS CodeStar.

Step 6: Add More Team Members

One of the benefits of an AWS CodeStar project is the simplified process for adding users and giving them access to project resources. Every AWS CodeStar project comes preconfigured with three different AWS CodeStar roles. Each role provides its own level of access to the project and its resources:

- **Owner**: Can add and remove team members, change the project dashboard, and delete the project.
- **Contributor**: Can change the project dashboard and contribute code if the code is stored in AWS CodeCommit, but cannot add or remove team members or delete the project. This is the role you should choose for most team members in an AWS CodeStar project.
- **Viewer**: Can view the project dashboard, project code if the code is stored in AWS CodeCommit, and the state of the project, but cannot move, add, or remove tiles from the project dashboard.

Important

If your project uses resources outside of AWS, for example a GitHub repository or issues in Atlassian JIRA, access to those resources are controlled by the resource provider, not AWS CodeStar. For more information, see the resource provider's documentation.

Anyone who has access to an AWS CodeStar project may be able to use the AWS CodeStar console to access resources that are outside of AWS but are related to that project.

AWS CodeStar does not automatically allow project team members to participate in any related AWS Cloud9 development environments for a project. To allow a team member to participate in a shared environment, see Share an AWS Cloud9 Environment with a Project Team Member.

For more information about teams and project roles, see Working with AWS CodeStar Teams.

To add a team member to an AWS CodeStar project (console)

1. Open the AWS CodeStar console at https://console.aws.amazon.com/codestar/.

   Choose the project.

2. In the navigation bar for the project, choose **Team**.

3. On the **Team members** page, choose **Add team member**.

4. In **Choose user**, do one of the following:

   - If an IAM user already exists for the person you want to add, choose the IAM user name from the list. **Note**
     Users who have already been added to another AWS CodeStar project will appear in the **AWS CodeStar users from other projects** list.

     On the **Add team member** tab, in **Project role**, choose the AWS CodeStar role (Owner, Contributor, or Viewer) for this user. This is an AWS CodeStar project-level role that can only be changed by an owner of the project. When applied to an IAM user, the role provides all appropriate permissions required to access AWS CodeStar project resources. It applies policies required for creating and managing Git credentials for code stored in AWS CodeCommit in IAM or uploading Amazon EC2 SSH keys for the user in IAM. **Important**
     You cannot provide or change the display name or email information for an IAM user unless you are signed in to the console as that user. For more information, see Manage Display Information for Your AWS CodeStar User Profile .

   Choose **Add**.

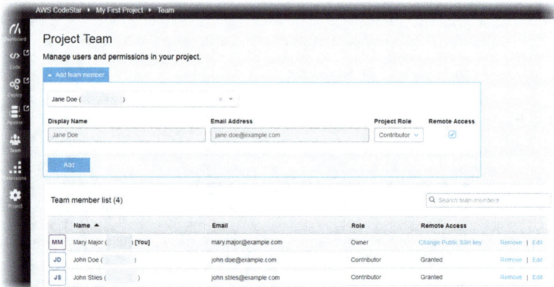

- If an IAM user does not exist for the person you want to add to the project, choose **Create new IAM user**. Fill in the IAM user name, AWS CodeStar display name, email address, and project role you want to apply to this new user, and choose **Create**.

Create IAM user ✖

Create an IAM user to add to your project.

IAM user name

DemoUser

Display Name

John Doe

Email

john.doe@example.com

Project role   **Remote access**

Viewer   ☐

Cancel   Create

You will be redirected to the IAM console to confirm user creation. Choose **Create user**, save the password information for that new user, and then choose **Close** to return to the AWS CodeStar console. The user will be automatically added to the project with the role you chose. **Note** For ease of management, at least one user should have the **Owner** role for the project.

5. Send the new team member the following information:

- Connection information for your AWS CodeStar project.
- If the source code is stored in AWS CodeCommit, Instructions for setting up access with Git credentials to the AWS CodeCommit repository from their local computers.
- Information about how the user can manage their display name, email address, and public Amazon EC2 SSH key, as described in Working with Your AWS CodeStar User Profile .
- One-time password and connection information, if the user is new to AWS and you created an IAM user for that person. The password will expire the first time the user logs on. The user must choose a new password.

Step 7: Clean Up

Congratulations! You've finished the Getting Started walkthrough for AWS CodeStar. If you don't want to continue to use this project and its resources, you should delete it so you can avoid any possible ongoing charges to your AWS account.

To delete a project in AWS CodeStar

1. Open the AWS CodeStar console at https://console.aws.amazon.com/codestar/.

2. Find the project in the list, and from the ellipsis menu, choose **Delete**.

   Alternatively, open the project, and in the navigation pane, choose **Project**. On the project details page, choose **Delete project**.

3. In the box next to **Type the following project ID to confirm**, type the ID of the project, and then choose **Delete**.

   Deleting a project can take several minutes. After it's deleted, the project no longer appears in the list of projects in the AWS CodeStar console. **Important**
   By default, when you delete a project, all resources listed under **Project resources** are deleted. If you clear the check box, the project resources are retained. For more information, go here.
   If your project uses resources outside of AWS (for example, a GitHub repository or issues in Atlassian JIRA), those resources are not deleted, even if you select the check box.
   Your project cannot be deleted if any AWS CodeStar managed policies have been manually attached to roles that are not IAM users. If you have attached your project's managed policies to a federated user's role, you must detach the policy before you can delete the project. For more information, see Detach an AWS CodeStar Managed Policy from the Federated User's Role.

Step 8: Ready Your Project for a Production Environment

After you have created your project, you are ready to create, test, and deploy code. Review the following considerations for maintaining your project in a production environment:

- You should regularly apply available patches and review security best practices for the dependencies used by your application. For a list of guidelines, see Security Best Practices for AWS CodeStar Resources.
- You should regularly monitor the environment settings suggested by the programming language specific to your project.

Next Steps

We suggest continuing to learn about AWS CodeStar by using the following resources:

- The Tutorial: Creating and Managing a Serverless Project in AWS CodeStar uses a project that creates and deploys a web service using logic in AWS Lambda and can be called by an API in Amazon API Gateway.
- AWS CodeStar Project Templates describes other types of projects you can create.
- Customize an AWS CodeStar Dashboard provides more information about customizing your projects' dashboards, integrating with JIRA, and more.
- Working with AWS CodeStar Teams provides more information about enabling others to help you work on your projects.

Tutorial: Creating and Managing a Serverless Project in AWS CodeStar

In this tutorial, you will use AWS CodeStar to create a project that uses the AWS Serverless Application Model (AWS SAM) to create and manage AWS resources for a web service hosted in AWS Lambda.

AWS CodeStar uses AWS SAM, which relies on AWS CloudFormation, to provide a simplified way of creating and managing supported AWS resources, including Amazon API Gateway APIs, AWS Lambda functions, and Amazon DynamoDB tables. (This project does not use any Amazon DynamoDB tables.)

For more information about AWS SAM, see AWS Serverless Application Model (AWS SAM) on GitHub.

Prerequisite: Complete the steps in Setting Up AWS CodeStar.

Note
Your AWS account may be charged for costs related to this tutorial, including costs for AWS services used by AWS CodeStar. For more information, see AWS CodeStar Pricing.

Topics

- Overview
- Step 1: Create the Project
- Step 2: Explore Project Resources
- Step 3: Test the Web Service
- Step 4: Set Up Your Local Workstation to Edit Project Code
- Step 5: Add Logic to the Web Service
- Step 6: Test the Enhanced Web Service
- Step 7: Add a Unit Test to the Web Service
- Step 8: View Unit Test Results
- Step 9: Clean Up
- Next Steps

Overview

In this tutorial, you will do the following:

1. Use AWS CodeStar to create a project that uses AWS SAM to build and deploy a Python-based web service. This web service is hosted in AWS Lambda and can be accessed through Amazon API Gateway.

2. Explore the project's main resources, which include:

   - The AWS CodeCommit repository where the project's source code is stored. This source code includes the web service's logic and defines related AWS resources.
   - The AWS CodePipeline pipeline that automates the building of the source code. This pipeline uses AWS SAM to create and deploy a function to AWS Lambda, create a related API in Amazon API Gateway, and connect the API to the function.
   - The function that is deployed to AWS Lambda.
   - The API that is created in Amazon API Gateway.

3. Manually test the web service to confirm that AWS CodeStar built and deployed the web service as expected.

4. Set up your local workstation to work with the project's source code.

5. Change the project's source code using your local workstation. You add a function to the project and then push your changes to the source code, which instructs AWS CodeStar to rebuild and redeploy the web service.

6. Manually test the web service again to confirm that AWS CodeStar rebuilt and redeployed as expected.

7. Write a unit test using your local workstation to replace some of your manual testing with an automated test. Push the unit test, which instructs AWS CodeStar to rebuild and redeploy the web service and run the unit test automatically.

8. View the results of the unit tests.

9. Clean up the project. This step is to keep AWS from charging your AWS account for costs related to this tutorial.

Step 1: Create the Project

In this step, you use the AWS CodeStar console to create a project. This project uses AWS SAM to create and deploy a Python-based web service that is hosted in AWS Lambda and can be accessed through Amazon API Gateway.

1. Sign in to the AWS Management Console and open the AWS CodeStar console, at https://console.aws.amazon.com/codestar/. **Note**
   You must sign in to the AWS Management Console using credentials associated with the IAM user you created or identified in Setting Up AWS CodeStar. This user must have the AWS managed policy named **AWSCodeStarFullAccess** attached.

2. Choose the AWS region where you want to create the project and its resources.

   For information about AWS regions where AWS CodeStar is available, see Regions and Endpoints in the *AWS General Reference*.

3. Choose **Create a new project** (or, if **Create a new project** is not displayed, **Start a new project**).

4. On the **Choose a project template** page::

   - For **Application category**, select **Web service**.
   - For **Programming languages**, select **Python**.
   - For **AWS services**, select **AWS Lambda**.

5. Choose the box that contains your selections.

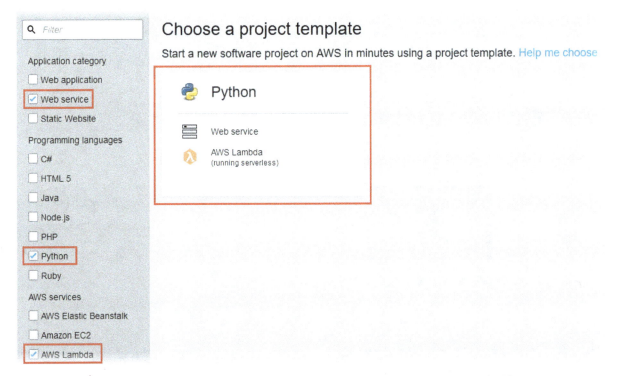

6. For **Project name**, type a name for the project (for example, **My SAM Project**). If you type a name different from the example, be sure to use it throughout this tutorial.

   For **Project ID**, AWS CodeStar chooses a related identifier for this project (for example, **my-sam-project**). If you see a different project ID, be sure to use it throughout this tutorial.

   Leave **AWS CodeCommit** selected, and do not change the **Repository name** value.

7. Choose **Next**.

8. Leave the **AWS CodeStar would like permission to administer AWS resources on your behalf** box selected, and then choose **Create Project**.

   If this is your first time using AWS CodeStar in this AWS region, then for **Display Name** and **Email**, type the display name and email address you want AWS CodeStar to use for your IAM user. Choose **Next**.

9. On the **Choose how you want to edit your project code** page, choose **Skip**. You set up your local workstation to edit the project's code in a later step.

10. Wait while AWS CodeStar creates the project. This might take several minutes. Do not proceed until you see **Welcome to My SAM Project!**.

Add tile

Welcome to My SAM Project!
Let us help you get started.

Learn about AWS CodeStar

Set up your team

Step 2: Explore Project Resources

In this step, you explore four of the project's AWS resources to understand how the project works.

- The AWS CodeCommit repository where the project's source code is stored. AWS CodeStar gives the repository the name **my-sam-project**, where **my-sam-project** is the name of the project.
- The AWS CodePipeline pipeline that uses AWS CodeBuild and AWS SAM to automate building and deploying the web service's Lambda function and API in API Gateway. AWS CodeStar gives the pipeline the name **my-sam-project--Pipeline**, where **my-sam-project** is the ID of the project.
- The Lambda function that contains the logic of the web service. AWS CodeStar gives the function the name **awscodestar-my-sam-project-lambda-HelloWorld-*RANDOM_ID***, where:
  - **my-sam-project** is the ID of the project.
  - **HelloWorld** is the function ID as specified in the `template.yaml` file in the AWS CodeCommit repository. You explore this file later.
  - *RANDOM_ID* is a random ID that AWS SAM assigns to the function to help ensure uniqueness.
- The API in API Gateway that makes it easier to call the Lambda function. AWS CodeStar gives the API the name **awscodestar-my-sam-project--lambda**, where **my-sam-project** is the ID of the project.

To explore the source code repository in AWS CodeCommit

1. With your project open in the AWS CodeStar console, on the side navigation bar, choose **Code**.

2. In the AWS CodeCommit console, on the **Code** page, the source code files for the project are displayed.

- `buildspec.yml`, which AWS CodePipeline instructs AWS CodeBuild to use during the build phase, to package the web service using AWS SAM.
- `index.py`, which contains the logic for the Lambda function. This function simply outputs the string `Hello World`, along with a timestamp in ISO format.
- `README.md`, which contains general information about the repository.
- `template.yml`, which AWS SAM uses to package the web service and create the API in API Gateway.

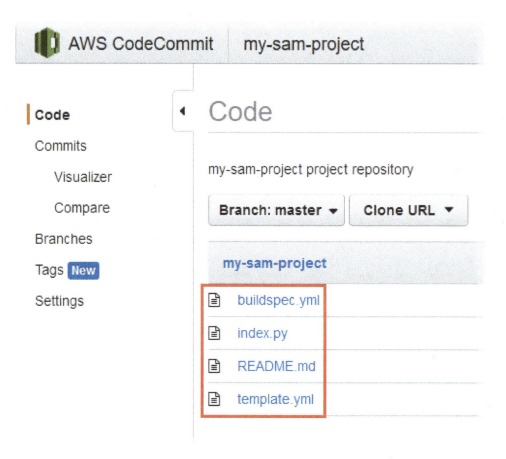

To view the contents of a file, simply choose it from the list.

For more information about using the AWS CodeCommit console, see the AWS CodeCommit User Guide.

To explore the pipeline in AWS CodePipeline

1. To view information about the pipeline, with your project open in the AWS CodeStar console, on the side navigation bar, choose **Dashboard**. On the **Continuous deployment** tile, you see the pipeline contains:

   - A **Source** stage for getting the source code from AWS CodeCommit.
   - A **Build** stage for building the source code with AWS CodeBuild.
   - A **Deploy** stage for deploying the built source code and AWS resources with AWS SAM.

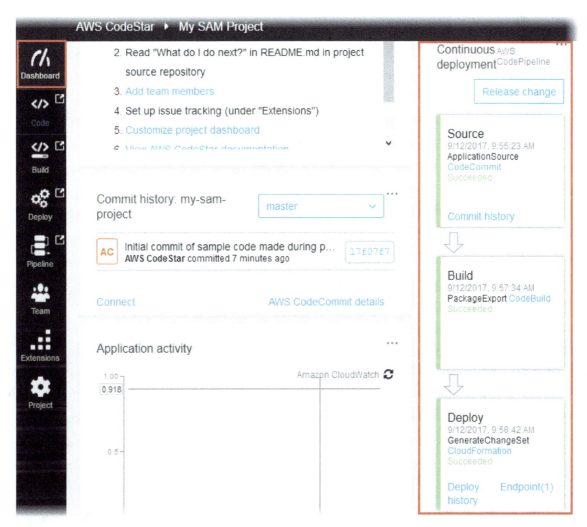

2. To view detailed information about the pipeline, on the **Continuous deployment** tile, choose the **AWS CodePipeline details** link or, on the side navigation bar, choose **Pipeline** to open the pipeline in the AWS CodePipeline console.

For information about using the AWS CodePipeline console, see the AWS CodePipeline User Guide.

To explore the function in Lambda

1. With your project open in the AWS CodeStar console, on the side navigation bar, choose **Project**.

2. In the **Project Resources** list, choose the link in the **ARN** column for the Lambda function.

The function's code is displayed in the Lambda console.

For information about using the Lambda console, see the AWS Lambda Developer Guide.

To explore the API in API Gateway

1. With your project open in the AWS CodeStar console, on the side navigation bar, choose **Project**.

2. In the **Project Resources** list, choose the link in the **ARN** column for the Amazon API Gateway API. Settings for the API are displayed in the API Gateway console.

For information about using the API Gateway console, see the API Gateway Developer Guide.

Step 3: Test the Web Service

In this step, you will test the web service that AWS CodeStar just built and deployed.

1. With your project still open from the previous step, on the side navigation bar, choose **Dashboard**.

2. On the **Continuous deployment** tile, make sure **Succeeded** is displayed for the **Source**, **Build**, and **Deploy** stages before you continue. This might take several minutes.

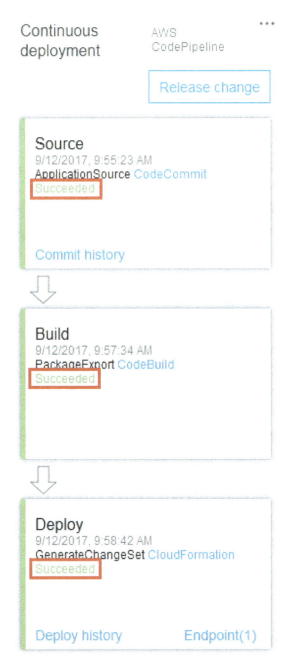

Note

If **Failed** is displayed for any of the stages, see the following for troubleshooting help:

For the **Source** stage, see Troubleshooting AWS CodeCommit in the *AWS CodeCommit User Guide*. For the **Build** stage, see Troubleshooting AWS CodeBuild in the *AWS CodeBuild User Guide*. For the **Deploy** stage, see Troubleshooting AWS CloudFormation in the *AWS CloudFormation User Guide*. For other issues, see Troubleshooting AWS CodeStar.

3. Choose the link on the **Application endpoints** tile. It should look like **https://*API_ID*.execute-api.*REGION_ID*.amazonaws.com/Prod/**, where:

- *API_ID* represents the ID that API Gateway assigned to the API.
- *REGION_ID* is the ID of the related AWS region.
- **Prod** is the name of the related API deployment stage in API Gateway.

On the new tab that opens in your web browser,.the web service displays the following response output:

1 {"output": "Hello World", "timestamp": "2017-08-30T15:53:42.682839"}

Step 4: Set Up Your Local Workstation to Edit Project Code

In this step, you will set up your local workstation to edit the source code in the AWS CodeStar project. Your local workstation can be a physical or virtual computer running macOS, Windows, or Linux.

1. With your project still open from the previous step, do one of the following:

   - If **You must connect to your project's repository before you can start working on the code** is displayed, choose the **Connect Tools** button.
   - In the side navigation pane, choose **Project**, and then choose the **Connect tools** button.

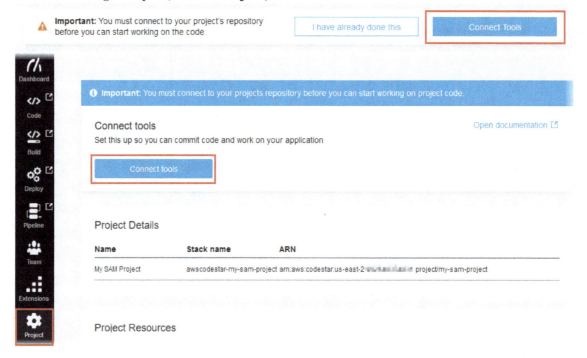

2. Choose the **Command line tools** tile.

   If you have Visual Studio or Eclipse installed, choose the **Visual Studio** or **Eclipse** tile instead, follow the instructions, and then skip to Step 5: Add Logic to the Web Service.

3. On the **Connect to your tools** page, for **Operating System**, choose the operating system running on your local workstation.

4. For **Connection Method**, choose **HTTPS**.

   We recommend that you choose **HTTPS** instead of **SSH** because HTTPS has fewer setup tasks. If you must use SSH, choose **SSH**, follow the instructions, and then skip to Step 5: Add Logic to the Web Service.

5. Follow the instructions to complete the following tasks:

   1. Set up Git on your local workstation.

   2. Use the IAM console to generate Git credentials for your IAM user.

   3. Clone the project's AWS CodeCommit repository onto your local workstation.

Step 5: Add Logic to the Web Service

In this step, you use your local workstation to add logic to the web service. Specifically, you add a Lambda function and then connect it to the API in API Gateway.

1. On your local workstation, go to the directory that contains the cloned source code repository.

2. In that directory, create a file named `hello.py`. Add the following code to the file, and then save the file:

```
1  import json
2
3  def handler(event, context):
4    data = {
5      'output': 'Hello ' + event["pathParameters"]["name"]
6    }
7    return {'statusCode': 200,
8      'body': json.dumps(data),
9      'headers': {'Content-Type': 'application/json'}}
```

The preceding code simply outputs the string `Hello` along with whatever string the caller sends to the function.

3. In the same directory, open the `template.yml` file. Add the following code to the end of the file, and then save the file:

```
1    Hello:
2      Type: AWS::Serverless::Function
3      Properties:
4        Handler: hello.handler
5        Runtime: python2.7
6        Role:
7          Fn::ImportValue:
8            !Join ['-', [!Ref 'ProjectId', !Ref 'AWS::Region', 'LambdaTrustRole']]
9        Events:
10          GetEvent:
11            Type: Api
12            Properties:
13              Path: /hello/{name}
14              Method: get
```

AWS SAM will use the preceding code to create a function in Lambda, add a new method and path to the API in API Gateway, and then connect this method and path to the new function. **Note** The indentation of the preceding code is important. If you don't add the code exactly it's shown, the project might not build correctly.

4. Use Git to add your file changes to the cloned repository's staging area by running the command `git add .` Do not forget the dot (`.`), which adds all changed files. **Note** If you are using Visual Studio or Eclipse instead of the command line, the instructions for using Git might be different. Consult the Visual Studio or Eclipse documentation.

5. Use Git to commit your staged files in the cloned repository by running the command `git commit -m "Added hello.py and updated template.yaml."`

6. Use Git to push your commit to the remote repository by running the `command git push`. **Note** You might be prompted for the user name and password IAM generated for you earlier. To keep from being prompted each time you interact with the remote repository, consider installing and configuring a Git credential manager. For example, on macOS or Linux you can run `git config credential.helper 'cache --timeout 900'` in the terminal to be prompted no sooner than every 15 minutes. Or you can run `git config credential.helper 'store --file ~/.git-credentials'` to never be prompted

again. Git will store your credentials in clear text in a plain file in your home directory. For more information, see Git Tools - Credential Storage on the Git website.

After AWS CodeStar detects the push, it instructs AWS CodePipeline to use AWS CodeBuild and AWS SAM to rebuild and redeploy the web service automatically.

AWS SAM gives the new function the name **awscodestar-my-sam-project-lambda-Hello-*RANDOM_ID***, where:

- **my-sam-project** is the ID of the project.
- **Hello** is the function ID as specified in the `template.yaml` file.
- *RANDOM_ID* is a random ID that AWS SAM assigns to the function for uniqueness.

Step 6: Test the Enhanced Web Service

In this step, you test the enhanced web service that AWS CodeStar built and deployed, based on the logic you added in the previous step.

1. With your project still open in the AWS CodeStar console, on the side navigation bar, choose **Dashboard**.

2. On the **Continuous deployment** tile, make sure the pipeline has run again and that **Succeeded** is displayed for the **Source**, **Build**, and **Deploy** stages before you continue. This might take several minutes.
   Note
   If **Failed** is displayed for any of the stages, see the following for troubleshooting help:
   For the **Source** stage, see Troubleshooting AWS CodeCommit in the *AWS CodeCommit User Guide.* For the **Build** stage, see Troubleshooting AWS CodeBuild in the *AWS CodeBuild User Guide.* For the **Deploy** stage, see Troubleshooting AWS CloudFormation in the *AWS CloudFormation User Guide.* For other issues, see Troubleshooting AWS CodeStar.

3. Choose the link on the **Application endpoints** tile. It should look like **https://*API_ID*.execute-api.*REGION_ID*.amazonaws.com/Prod/**, where:

   - *API_ID* represents the ID that API Gateway assigned to the API.
   - *REGION_ID* is the ID of the related AWS region.
   - **Prod** is the name of the related API deployment stage in API Gateway.

   On the new tab that opens in your web browser, the web service displays the following response output:

   ```
   1 {"output": "Hello World", "timestamp": "2017-08-30T15:53:42.682839"}
   ```

4. In the tab's address box, add the path **/hello/** and your first name to the end of the URL and then press **Enter**. For example, **https://*API_ID*.execute-api.*REGION_ID*.amazonaws.com/Prod/hello/*YOUR_FIRST_NAME***.

If your first name is Mary, the web service displays the following response output:

```
1 {"output": "Hello Mary"}
```

Step 7: Add a Unit Test to the Web Service

In this step, you use your local workstation to add a test that AWS CodeStar runs automatically on the web service. This test replaces the manual testing you did earlier.

1. On your local workstation, go to the directory that contains the cloned source code repository.

2. In that directory, create a file named `hello_test.py`. Add the following code to the file, and then save the file:

```
1 from hello import handler
2
3 def test_hello_handler():
4
5   event = {
6     'pathParameters': {
7       'name': 'testname'
8     }
9   }
10
11   context = {}
12
13   expected = {
14     'body': '{"output": "Hello testname"}',
15     'headers': {
16       'Content-Type': 'application/json'
17     },
18     'statusCode': 200
19   }
20
21   assert handler(event, context) == expected
```

This test checks whether the output of the Lambda function is in the expected format. If so, the test succeeds. Otherwise, the test fails.

3. In the same directory, open the `buildspec.yml` file. Replace the file's contents with the following code, and then save the file:

```
1 version: 0.2
2
3 phases:
4
5   install:
6     commands:
7       - pip install pytest
8
9   pre_build:
10     commands:
11       - pytest
12
13   build:
14     commands:
15       - aws cloudformation package --template template.yml --s3-bucket $S3_BUCKET --output-
           template template-export.json
16
17 artifacts:
18   type: zip
19   files:
20     - template-export.json
```

This build specification instructs AWS CodeBuild to install pytest, the Python test framework, into its build environment. AWS CodeBuild uses pytest to run the unit test. The rest of the build specification is the same as before.

4. Use Git to push these changes to the remote repository.

```
1 git add .
```

```
2
3 git commit -m "Added hello_test.py and updated buildspec.yml."
4
5 git push
```

Step 8: View Unit Test Results

In this step, you see whether the unit test succeeded or failed.

1. With your project still open in the AWS CodeStar console, on the side navigation bar, choose **Dashboard**.

2. On the **Continuous deployment** tile, make sure the pipeline has run again before you continue. This might take several minutes.

   If the unit test was successful, **Succeeded** is displayed for the **Build** stage. If the unit test failed, **Failed** is displayed.

3. To view the unit test result details, on the **Continuous deployment** tile, choose the **CodeBuild** link in the **Build** stage.

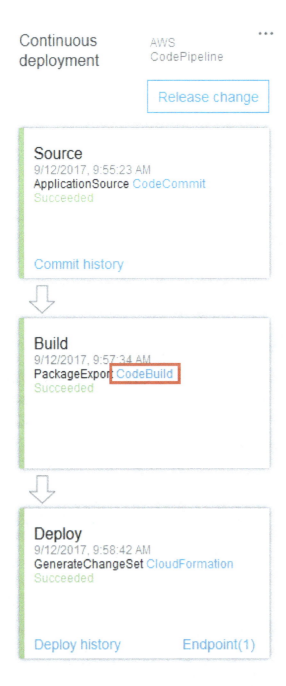

Continuous
deployment

AWS
CodePipeline

•••

Release change

Source
9/12/2017, 9:55:23 AM
ApplicationSource CodeCommit
Succeeded

Commit history

Build
9/12/2017, 9:57:34 AM
PackageExport CodeBuild
Succeeded

Deploy
9/12/2017, 9:58:42 AM
GenerateChangeSet CloudFormation
Succeeded

Deploy history   Endpoint(1)

4. In the AWS CodeBuild console, on the **Build Project: my-sam-project** page, in **Build history**, choose the link in the **Build run** column of the table.

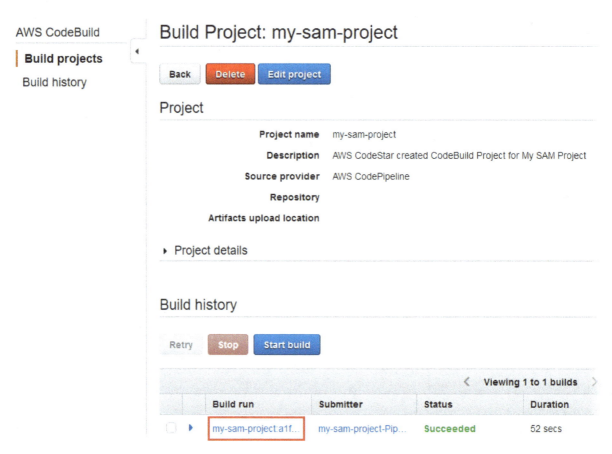

5. On the **my-sam-project:**_BUILD__ID_ page, in **Build logs**, choose the **View entire log** link.

Phase details

	Name	Status	Duration
▶	SUBMITTED	Succeeded	
▶	PROVISIONING	Succeeded	25 secs
▶	DOWNLOAD_SOURCE	Succeeded	22 secs
▶	INSTALL	Succeeded	
▶	PRE_BUILD	Succeeded	
▶	BUILD	Succeeded	
▶	POST_BUILD	Succeeded	
▶	UPLOAD_ARTIFACTS	Succeeded	
▶	FINALIZING	Succeeded	5 secs
▶	COMPLETED	Succeeded	

Build logs

Showing the last 20 lines of build log below. View entire log

```
[Container] 2017/09/12 16:56:20 Phase context status code: Message:
[Container] 2017/09/12 16:56:20 Entering phase BUILD
```

42

6. In the Amazon CloudWatch Logs console, look in the log output for a test result similar to the following. In the following test result, the test passed:

```
1  ...
2  ============================ test session starts ============================
3  platform linux2 -- Python 2.7.12, pytest-3.2.1, py-1.4.34, pluggy-0.4.0
4  rootdir: /codebuild/output/src123456789/src, inifile:
5  collected 1 item
6
7  hello_test.py .
8
9  ========================= 1 passed in 0.01 seconds =========================
10 ...
```

If the test failed, there should be details in the log output to help you troubleshoot the failure.

Step 9: Clean Up

In this step, you clean up the project to avoid ongoing charges related to this project.

If you want to keep using this project, you can skip this step, but your AWS account might continue to be charged.

1. With your project still open in the AWS CodeStar console, on the side navigation bar, choose **Project**.

2. Choose **Delete project**.

3. Type the name of the project, keep the **Delete associated resources along with AWS CodeStar project** box selected, and then choose **Delete**. **Important**
   If you clear this box, the project record will be deleted from AWS CodeStar, but many of the project's AWS resources will remain, and your AWS account might be charged for ongoing related costs.

An Amazon S3 bucket that AWS CodeStar created for this project might still remain. To delete this remaining bucket:

1. Open the AWS CodeCommit console, at https://console.aws.amazon.com/s3/.

2. In the list of buckets, choose the icon next to **aws-codestar-*REGION_ID*-*ACCOUNT_ID*-my-sam-project--pipe**, where:
   - *REGION_ID* is the ID of the AWS region for the project you just deleted.
   - *ACCOUNT_ID* is your AWS account ID.
   - **my-sam-project** is the ID of the project you just deleted.

3. Choose **Empty Bucket**. Type the name of the bucket, and then choose **Confirm**.

4. Choose **Delete Bucket**. Type the name of the bucket, and then choose **Confirm**.

Next Steps

Now that you have completed this tutorial, we suggest you review the following resources:

- The Getting Started with AWS CodeStar walkthrough uses a project that creates and deploys a Node.js-based web application running on an Amazon EC2 instance.
- AWS CodeStar Project Templates describes other types of projects you can create.
- Customize an AWS CodeStar Dashboard shows you how to customize your projects' dashboards, integrate with JIRA, and more.
- Working with AWS CodeStar Teams shows you how others can help you work on your projects.

AWS CodeStar Project Templates

You can use an AWS CodeStar project template to quickly configure AWS CodeStar to support your development project. These preconfigured AWS CloudFormation templates create projects based on your choices. They include support for development projects like websites, web services, microservices, Alexa skills, and more. You can use the search box or the filter bar to find a template.

Topics

- How Do I Choose the Right Template?
- Web Application
- Web Service
- Amazon Alexa Skill
- Use AWS CodeStar Templates with Built-in Unit Testing

How Do I Choose the Right Template?

Each AWS CodeStar project template includes the supported programming language in its title and description. The template name also indicates whether your project is hosted on servers in the cloud (Amazon EC2, either in a managed application environment (AWS Elastic Beanstalk) or that you manage yourself) or run serverless (without Amazon EC2 instances, for example on AWS Lambda). If you see two AWS CodeStar project templates that look the same, check the description and the service bar to determine the differences.

After you choose an AWS CodeStar project template, the page displays a list of resources to be created for the project. All of these resources are configured for you. You do not have to perform any manual configuration to get started with your project. If your project template includes Amazon EC2 instances, you can choose **Edit Amazon EC2 Configuration** to modify your configuration. Some of these choices, such as instance type, might affect the cost of your project. For more information, see Create a Project in AWS CodeStar and Pricing.

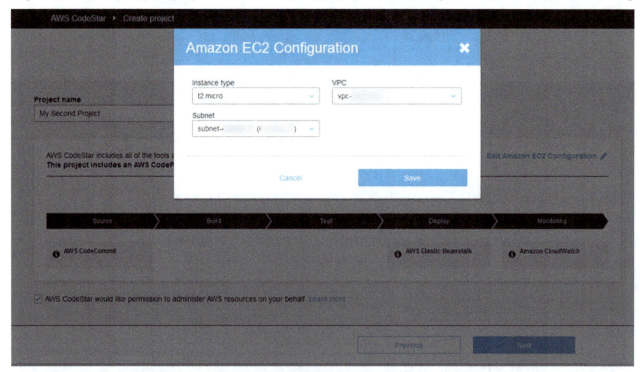

Many of the AWS CodeStar project templates allow you to choose from a variety of options to host your web application or service in the cloud. All options offer high availability and scaling. The option you choose is configured when the project is created. You don't have to worry about configuring interoperation or setting permissions. The following table can help you determine the best fit for your software project.

Which hosting option is right for my AWS CodeStar project?

AWS Elastic Beanstalk	Amazon EC2 with AWS CodeDeploy	AWS Lambda
Automated deployments to Amazon EC2 instances.	Automated deployments to Amazon EC2 instances.	Serverless (no servers or instances to manage or administer).
Automated management of capacity and load balancing.	Flexible deployment to any instance.	AWS CodeBuild configured to build your artifacts automatically.
Team member access to Amazon EC2 instances (if your project owner allows it).	Team member access to Amazon EC2 instances (if your project owner allows it).	Amazon API Gateway configured automatically as a Lambda proxy for GET and POST calls.
End-to-end application management solution.	Building block service focused on deploying and updating software.	Code executed in response to events.

After your project is created, you can view the sample source code included in your project, including a readme file that provides details of files and directories. This readme file also includes suggestions for how to get started with the sample code.

Web Application

The AWS CodeStar project templates in this category support development in Ruby, Java, ASP.NET, PHP, and more. A source repository and continuous delivery pipeline is configured for you automatically, along with a sample application that you can use to evaluate the AWS CodeStar project. You can choose AWS services to use for your application.

All web application projects include the following resources:

- A source code repository in AWS CodeCommit or GitHub.
- A continuous deployment pipeline in AWS CodePipeline.
- A CPU utilization monitor for Amazon EC2 instances (Amazon EC2 and AWS Elastic Beanstalk projects) or an Invocations and Errors monitor (AWS Lambda projects) in Amazon CloudWatch.
- Project roles and associated policies in IAM. Policies are applied automatically to IAM users when you add those users to your project team.
- Sample code for your project, including a README.md with details of the sample.

If you choose an AWS CodeStar project template that uses Lambda, your project also includes the following resources:

- A build server and environment in AWS CodeBuild.
- A sample function in Lambda.
- A RESTful API that exposes the Lambda function in Amazon API Gateway.
- Roles for job workers in IAM.

If you chose to create a project with AWS Lambda, you can add resources to your AWS CodeStar project by editing the template.yaml file that is included in the sample code for Lambda projects. Configurable resources include:

- Applications and deployment groups in AWS CodeDeploy.
- Applications and environments in AWS Elastic Beanstalk.

- Stages and actions in a pipeline in AWS CodePipeline.
- Events in Amazon CloudWatch.
- Build projects in AWS CodeBuild.

Web Service

This template supports development in Ruby, Java, ASP.NET, PHP, and more. A source repository, build server, and continuous delivery pipeline are configured for you automatically, along with CloudWatch metrics. This template also includes some sample code that you can use to help evaluate the AWS CodeStar project and its resources.

All web service projects include the following resources:

- A source code repository in AWS CodeCommit or GitHub.
- A continuous deployment pipeline in AWS CodePipeline.
- A CPU utilization monitor for Amazon EC2 instances (Amazon EC2 and AWS Elastic Beanstalk projects) or an Invocations and Errors monitor (AWS Lambda projects) in Amazon CloudWatch.
- Sample code for your project, including a README.md with details of the sample.

If you choose a AWS CodeStar project template that uses Lambda, your project also includes the following resources:

- A build server and environment in AWS CodeBuild .
- A sample function in Lambda.
- A RESTful API that exposes the Lambda function in Amazon API Gateway.
- Roles for job workers in IAM.

To view application activity in an AWS CodeStar project template that uses Lambda, you must first invoke the function by choosing to visit the host. The host link appears on the **Continuous deployment** tile of your project.

If you chose to create a project with AWS Lambda, you can add resources to your AWS CodeStar project by editing the template.yaml file that is included in the sample code for Lambda projects. Configurable resources include:

- Applications and deployment groups in AWS CodeDeploy.
- Applications and environments in AWS Elastic Beanstalk.
- Stages and actions in a pipeline in AWS CodePipeline.
- Events in Amazon CloudWatch.
- Build projects in AWS CodeBuild.

Amazon Alexa Skill

Choose this template if you want a project for a AWS Lambda function based on an Alexa skills blueprint for Amazon Alexa. The function returns an Amazon Resource Name (ARN) that you can use as a service endpoint for your Alexa skill when you configure it in the Alexa Developer Portal. For more information, see Creating an AWS Lambda Function for a Custom Skill.

Note
Lambda functions for Alexa skills are supported in the US East (N. Virginia) and EU (Ireland) Regions only.

All Alexa skill projects include the following resources:

- A source code repository in AWS CodeCommit or GitHub.
- A continuous deployment pipeline in AWS CodePipeline.
- An Invocations and Errors monitor in Amazon CloudWatch.
- Sample code for your project, including a README.md with details of the sample.
- A build server and environment in AWS CodeBuild.

- A sample function in Lambda.
- A RESTful API that exposes the Lambda function in Amazon API Gateway.
- Roles for job workers in IAM.

To view application activity in an AWS CodeStar project template that uses Lambda, you must first invoke the function by choosing to visit the host. The host link appears on the **Continuous deployment** tile of your project.

You can add resources to your AWS CodeStar project by editing the template.yaml file that is included in the sample code for Lambda projects. You can configure these resources:

- Applications and deployment groups in AWS CodeDeploy.
- Applications and environments in AWS Elastic Beanstalk.
- Stages and actions in a pipeline in AWS CodePipeline.
- Events in Amazon CloudWatch.
- Build projects in AWS CodeBuild.

Use AWS CodeStar Templates with Built-in Unit Testing

Most AWS CodeStar project templates come preconfigured with a unit testing framework and sample unit tests (in all but PHP, static HTML, and Alexa skill project templates). This enables you to quickly include unit testing in your project's included build process. Source code for these tests can be found in your project's source repository. Unit testing details can be found in the README file for your selected template.

You can also add unit testing manually by modifying the buildspec.yml file in your project's source code repository. For an example for the Python programming language, see Step 7: Add a Unit Test to the Web Service.

AWS CodeStar Best Practices

AWS CodeStar is integrated with a number of products and services. The following sections describe best practices for AWS CodeStar and these related products and services.

Topics

- Security Best Practices for AWS CodeStar Resources
- Monitoring and Logging Best Practices for AWS CodePipeline Resources

Security Best Practices for AWS CodeStar Resources

You should regularly apply available patches and review security best practices for the dependencies used by your application. Use these security best practices to update your sample code and maintain your project in a production environment:

- Track ongoing security announcements and updates specific to your framework.
- Before deploying your project, follow the documented best practices developed for your framework.
- Review dependencies for your framework on a regular basis and update as needed.
- Each AWS CodeStar template contains configuration instructions specific to your programming language. See the README.md file in your project's source repository for details.

Monitoring and Logging Best Practices for AWS CodePipeline Resources

You can use logging features in AWS to determine the actions users have taken in your account and the resources that were used. The log files show:

- The time and date of actions.
- The source IP address for an action.
- Which actions failed due to inadequate permissions.

AWS CloudTrail can be used to log AWS API calls and related events made by or on behalf of an AWS account. For more information, see Logging AWS CodeStar API Calls with AWS CloudTrail.

Working with Projects in AWS CodeStar

When you use an AWS CodeStar project template, you can quickly create a project that is already configured with the resources you need, including:

- Source repository.
- Build environment.
- Deployment and hosting resources.
- Programming language.

The template even includes sample source code so you can start working with your project right away.

After you have a project, you can start working with it by adding or removing resources, customizing your project dashboard, and monitoring progress.

The following diagram illustrates a basic workflow in an AWS CodeStar project.

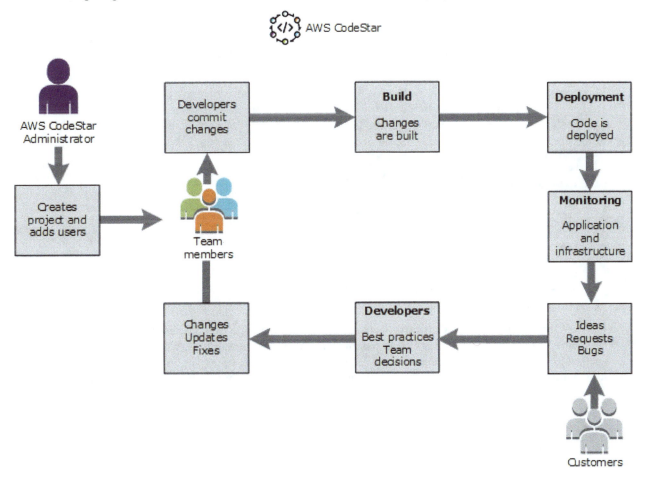

A developer with the **AWSCodeStarFullAccess** policy applied creates a project and adds team members to it. Together they write, build, test, and deploy code. The project dashboard provides tools that can be used in real time to view application activity and monitor builds, the flow of code through the deployment pipeline, and more. The team uses the team wiki tile to share information, best practices, and links. They integrate their issue-tracking software to help them track progress and tasks. As customers provide requests, information, and ideas, the team adds this information to the project and integrates it into their project planning and development. As the project grows, the team adds more team members to support their growing code base.

Create a Project in AWS CodeStar

You use the AWS CodeStar console to create a project. If you use a project template, it sets up the required resources. It also includes sample code you can use to start coding and to understand how the project resources work together.

To create a project, sign in to the AWS Management Console with an IAM user that has the **AWSCodeStar-FullAccess** policy or equivalent permissions. For more information, see Setting Up AWS CodeStar.

Note
You must complete the steps in Setting Up AWS CodeStar before you can complete the procedures in this topic.

Create a Project in AWS CodeStar

Use the AWS CodeStar console to create a project.

To create a project in AWS CodeStar

1. Sign in to the AWS Management Console, and then open the AWS CodeStar console at https://console.aws.amazon.com/codestar/.

   Make sure that you are signed in to the AWS region where you want to create the project and its resources. For example, to create a project in US East (Ohio), make sure you have that region selected. For information about AWS regions where AWS CodeStar is available, see Regions and Endpoints in the *AWS General Reference* .

2. On the **AWS CodeStar** page, choose **Create a new project**. (If you are the first user to create a project, choose **Start a project**.)

3. On the **Choose a project template** page, choose the project type from the list of AWS CodeStar project templates. You can use the filter bar to narrow your choices. For example, for a web application project written in Node.js that will be deployed to Amazon EC2 instances, select the **Web application**, **Node.js**, and **Amazon EC2** check boxes. Then choose from the templates available for that set of options.

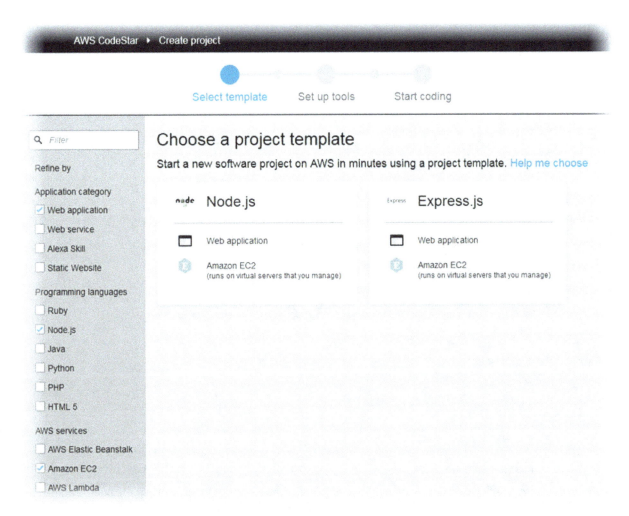

For more information, see AWS CodeStar Project Templates.

4. In **Project name**, type a name for the project, such as *My First Project*. The ID for the project is derived from this project name, but is limited to 15 characters.

For example, the default ID for a project named *My First Project* is *my-first-projec*. This project ID is the basis for the names of all resources associated with the project. For example, AWS CodeStar uses this project ID as part of the URL for your code repository as well as the names of related security access roles and policies in IAM. After the project is created, the project ID cannot be changed, so make sure you are okay with this project ID. To edit the project ID before you create the project, choose **Edit**.

For information about the limits on project names and project IDs, see Limits in AWS CodeStar. **Note** Project IDs must be unique for your AWS account within an AWS region.

Project details

Project name

My First Project

Project ID ⓘ   Edit

my-first-projec

Which repository do you want to use?

AWS CodeStar will store the project's source code with the service you choose here.

AWS CodeCommit
Highly available Git source control from AWS.
Includes encryption, IAM integration, and more.

GitHub
Creates a GitHub source repository for this project. Requires an existing GitHub account.

Repository name*

My-First-Project

Previous   Next

5. Choose the repository provider to store this project's source code with: **AWS CodeCommit** or **GitHub**.

6. If you chose **AWS CodeCommit**, for **Repository name**, accept the default AWS CodeCommit repository name that AWS CodeStar suggests, or type a different AWS CodeCommit repository name of your choice. Then skip ahead to step 8 in this procedure.

7. If you chose **GitHub**, then choose **Connect with GitHub**.

    1. If the **Sign in to GitHub** page is displayed, type your GitHub username or email address and password, and then choose **Sign in**. **Note**
    To complete this page, you must have a GitHub account. For more information, see Join GitHub on the GitHub website.

    2. If the **Two-factor authentication** page displays, for **Authentication code**, type the code that GitHub sends you. Then choose **Verify**.

    3. On the **Authorize AWS CodeStar** page, choose **Authorize**. **Note**
    When you choose **Authorize**, you allow AWS CodeStar to create a GitHub repository for your personal GitHub account, or for any GitHub organization where you have permissions (which is marked with a green check icon in **Organization access**).
    To add a GitHub organization to the **Organization access** list, ask one of the organization's owners to invite you to the organization by following the instructions in Inviting users to join your organization on the GitHub Help website. After you join the organization, refresh the **Authorize AWS CodeStar** page to see the organization in the list.
    To get permissions to authorize a GitHub organization that is in the list but does not have a green check icon, choose **Grant**. If you see **Request** instead, choose it, and then ask one of the organization's owners to allow AWS CodeStar to create a GitHub repository in the organization by following the instructions in Approving OAuth Apps for your organization on the GitHub Help website. After the owner does this, refresh the **Authorize AWS CodeStar** page to see the **Grant** button.

4. For **Owner**, choose the GitHub organization or your personal GitHub account that you want AWS CodeStar to create the GitHub repository for.

5. For **Repository name**, accept the default GitHub repository name that AWS CodeStar suggests, or type a different GitHub repository name of your choice.

6. Choose **Public repository** or **Private repository** to make the GitHub repository public or private. **Note**
   Depending on your GitHub account type, GitHub may not allow you to create a private repository. For more information, see GitHub Pricing on the GitHub website.

7. For **Repository description**, provide an optional description for the GitHub repository.

8. Choose **Next**.

9. Review the resources and configuration details. Choose **Edit Amazon EC2 Configuration** (where available) if your project will deploy to Amazon EC2 instances and you want to make changes. For example, you can choose from available instance types for your project. **Note**
   Different Amazon EC2 instance types provide different levels of computing power and might have different associated costs. For more information, see Amazon EC2 Instance Types and Amazon EC2 Pricing.
   If you have more than one virtual private cloud (VPC) or multiple subnets created in Amazon Virtual Private Cloud, you can also choose the VPC and subnet to use. However, if you choose an Amazon EC2 instance type that is not supported on dedicated instances, you cannot choose a VPC whose instance tenancy is set to **Dedicated**.
   For more information, see What Is Amazon VPC? and Dedicated Instance Basics.

10. Leave the **AWS CodeStar would like permission to administer AWS resources on your behalf** check box selected. If this box is not selected, you will not be able to create a project. For more information about the service role, the policy, and its permissions, see AWS CodeStar Service Role Policy and Permissions.

    Choose **Next** or **Create project**. (The displayed choice depends on your project template.)

11. In **Choose an Amazon EC2 Key Pair**, choose the Amazon EC2 key pair you created in Step 4: Create an Amazon EC2 Key Pair for AWS CodeStar Projects in *Setting Up*. Select **I acknowledge that I have access to the private key file for this key pair**, and then choose **Create project**.

12. It might take a few minutes to create the project (including the repository). After your project has a

repository, you can use the **Set up tools** page to configure access to it, or you can choose **Skip** and configure access later. After your project has been created, you will see a **Welcome** tile that contains useful links. You can use these links to optionally configure other items, such as your user profile in AWS CodeStar.

While your project is being created, you can add team members or configure access to your project repository from the command line or your favorite IDE.

Use an IDE with AWS CodeStar

When you integrate an integrated development environment (IDE) with AWS CodeStar, you can continue to write and develop code in your preferred environment. The changes you make will be included in the AWS CodeStar project each time you commit and push your code.

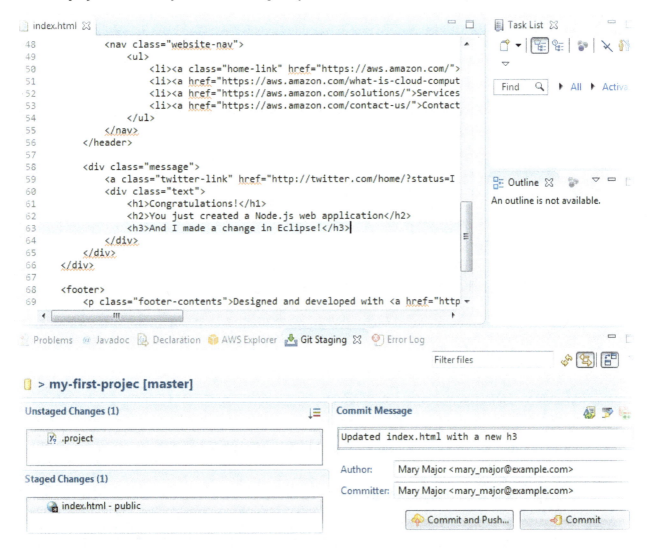

Topics

- Use AWS Cloud9 with AWS CodeStar
- Use Eclipse with AWS CodeStar
- Use Visual Studio with AWS CodeStar

Use AWS Cloud9 with AWS CodeStar

You can use AWS Cloud9 to make code changes and develop software in an AWS CodeStar project. AWS Cloud9 is an online IDE, which you access through your web browser. The IDE offers a rich code editing experience with support for several programming languages and runtime debuggers, as well as a built-in terminal. You can configure the IDE to your preferences. These include switching color themes, binding shortcut keys, enabling programming language-specific syntax coloring and code formatting, and more. In the background, an Amazon EC2 instance hosts an AWS Cloud9 development environment. This environment provides the AWS Cloud9 IDE and access to the AWS CodeStar project's code files. For more information, see the *AWS Cloud9 User Guide*.

You can use the AWS CodeStar console or AWS Cloud9 console to create AWS Cloud9 development environments for projects that store their code in AWS CodeCommit. For AWS CodeStar projects that store their code in GitHub, you can only use the AWS Cloud9 console. This topic describes how to use both consoles.

Topics

- Create an AWS Cloud9 Environment for a Project
- Open an AWS Cloud9 Environment for a Project
- Share an AWS Cloud9 Environment with a Project Team Member
- Delete an AWS Cloud9 Environment from a Project
- Use GitHub with AWS Cloud9
- Additional Resources

Create an AWS Cloud9 Environment for a Project

You can create an AWS Cloud9 development environment for an existing or new project in AWS CodeStar, as follows:

1. Do one of the following:

   - If you have an existing project, open the project in the AWS CodeStar console. On the side navigation bar, choose **IDE**. Choose **Create new environment**, and then skip ahead to step 2 in this procedure.
   Important
   If the project's source code is stored in GitHub, you won't see **IDE** on the side navigation bar. However, you can use the AWS Cloud9 console to create a development environment, open the new environment, and then connect it to the existing project's GitHub repository. To do this, skip the rest of this procedure and see Use GitHub with AWS Cloud9.
   If the project is in an AWS Region where AWS Cloud9 isn't supported, you won't see **IDE** on the side navigation bar. However, you can use the AWS Cloud9 console to create a development environment, open the new environment, and then connect it to the existing project's AWS CodeCommit repository. To do this, skip the rest of this procedure and see Creating an Environment, Opening an Environment, and the AWS CodeCommit Sample in the *AWS Cloud9 User Guide*. See also the list of supported AWS Regions for AWS Cloud9 in the *Amazon Web Services General Reference*.

   - If you have not yet created a project, follow the steps in Create a Project. When the create project wizard gets to the **Set up tools** page, for **Pick how you want to edit your code**, choose **Cloud9**. Choose **Next**, and then skip ahead to step 2 in this procedure. **Important**
   If you choose to store the project's source code in GitHub, on the **Set up tools** page, you will see **Connect to your source repository** instead of **Pick how you want to edit your code**, and there are no options here to choose AWS Cloud9. However, after AWS CodeStar creates the project, you can use the AWS Cloud9 console to create a development environment, open the new environment, and then connect it to the new project's GitHub repository. To do this, skip the rest of this procedure and see Use GitHub with AWS Cloud9.
   If the project is in an AWS Region where AWS Cloud9 is not supported, on the **Set up tools** page, you won't see any options to choose AWS Cloud9. However, you can use the AWS Cloud9 console to create a development environment, open the new environment, and then connect it to the existing

project's AWS CodeCommit repository. To do this, skip the rest of this procedure and see Creating an Environment, Opening an Environment, and the AWS CodeCommit Sample in the *AWS Cloud9 User Guide*. See also the list of supported AWS Regions for AWS Cloud9 in the *Amazon Web Services General Reference*.

2. To change the default type of Amazon EC2 instance to host the environment, for **Pick an instance type for the IDE (not your overall project)**, choose the instance type.

3. To change the default environment name, add a description for the environment, or both, expand **Environment name and description**, and then change the settings. **Note** Environment names must be unique per user.

4. AWS Cloud9 uses Amazon Virtual Private Cloud (Amazon VPC) in your AWS account to communicate with the instance. Depending on how Amazon VPC is set up in your AWS account, do one of the following.

[See the AWS documentation website for more details]

For more information, see Amazon Virtual Private Cloud (Amazon VPC) Settings for an AWS Cloud9 EC2 Development Environment in the *AWS Cloud9 User Guide*.

1. To change the default time period when AWS Cloud9 shuts down the environment after it has not been used, expand **Cost-saving options**, and then change the setting.

2. Choose **Next**.

To open the environment, see Open an AWS Cloud9 Environment for a Project.

You can create more than one environment for a project by following the preceding steps. For example, you might want to use one environment to work on one portion of the code, and use another environment to work on the same portion of the code with different settings—or you may want to work on another portion of the code altogether.

Open an AWS Cloud9 Environment for a Project

To open an existing AWS Cloud9 development environment that you created for a project in AWS CodeStar, do the following:

1. With the project open in the AWS CodeStar console, on the side navigation bar, choose **IDE. Important** If the project's source code is stored in GitHub, you won't see **IDE** on the side navigation bar. However, you can use the AWS Cloud9 console to open an existing environment. To do this, skip the rest of this procedure and see Opening an Environment in the *AWS Cloud9 User Guide*. See also Use GitHub with AWS Cloud9.

2. For **My Cloud9 environments** or **Shared Cloud9 environments**, choose **Open IDE** for the environment you want to open.

AWS Cloud9 opens the environment and displays the AWS Cloud9 IDE. You can use the IDE to begin working with code in the project's AWS CodeCommit repository right away. For more information, see The Environment Window, The Editor, Tabs, and Panes, and The Terminal in the *AWS Cloud9 User Guide*. See also Basic Git Commands in the *AWS CodeCommit User Guide*.

Share an AWS Cloud9 Environment with a Project Team Member

After you create an AWS Cloud9 development environment for a project in AWS CodeStar, you can invite other users across your AWS account—including project team members—to access that same environment. This is especially useful for pair programming, where two programmers take turns coding and giving advice about the same code while sitting at the same workstation or through screen sharing. Environment members can use the shared AWS Cloud9 IDE to see each member's code changes highlighted within the code editor, and to text chat with other members while coding.

Adding a team member to a project doesn't automatically allow that member to participate in any related AWS Cloud9 development environments for the project. To invite a project team member to access an environment for a project, see About Environment Member Access Roles and Invite an IAM User to Your Environment in the *AWS Cloud9 User Guide*. When you invite a project team member to access an environment for a project, the AWS CodeStar console displays the environment to that team member. The environment is displayed in the **Shared Cloud9 environments** list on the **IDE** tab in the AWS CodeStar console for the project. To display this list, have the team member open the project in the console, and then choose **IDE** in the side navigation bar.

Important
If the project's source code is stored in GitHub, you won't see **IDE** on the side navigation bar. However, you can use the AWS Cloud9 console to invite other users across your AWS account—including project team members—to access an environment. To do this, see Use GitHub with AWS Cloud9 in this guide, and see About Environment Member Access Roles and Invite an IAM User to Your Environment in the *AWS Cloud9 User Guide*.

You can also invite a user who is not a project team member to access an environment. For example, you might want a user to work on a project's code but have no other access to that project. To invite this type of user, see About Environment Member Access Roles and Invite an IAM User to Your Environment in the *AWS Cloud9 User Guide*. When you invite a user who is not a project team member to access an environment for a project, that user can use the AWS Cloud9 console to access the environment. For more information, see Open an Environment in the *AWS Cloud9 User Guide*.

Delete an AWS Cloud9 Environment from a Project

When you delete a project from AWS CodeStar and you choose to also delete all related AWS resources for that project, all related AWS Cloud9 development environments that were created with the AWS CodeStar console are also deleted and cannot be recovered. However, you can delete an existing development environment from a project without deleting the project itself, as follows:

1. With the project open in the AWS CodeStar console, choose **IDE** in the side navigation bar. **Important** If the project's source code is stored in GitHub, you won't see **IDE** on the side navigation bar. However, you can use the AWS Cloud9 console to delete a development environment. To do this, skip the rest of this procedure and see Deleting an Environment in the *AWS Cloud9 User Guide*.

2. Inside of the tile for the environment you want to delete, choose the ellipses (**...**).

3. Type the development environment's name, and then choose **Delete. Warning** Deleting a development environment cannot be undone. All uncommitted code changes in the environment will be lost.

Use GitHub with AWS Cloud9

For AWS CodeStar projects that have their source code stored in GitHub, the AWS CodeStar console doesn't support working with AWS Cloud9 development environments directly. However, you can use the AWS Cloud9 console to work with source code in GitHub repositories, as follows:

1. Use the AWS Cloud9 console to create an AWS Cloud9 development environment, if one doesn't already exist. To do this, see Creating an Environment in the *AWS Cloud9 User Guide*.

2. Use the AWS Cloud9 console to open the development environment, if AWS Cloud9 doesn't open it automatically. To do this, see Opening an Environment in the *AWS Cloud9 User Guide*.

3. When you or AWS Cloud9 open the development environment, the AWS Cloud9 IDE is displayed. In the IDE, use a terminal session to connect to the GitHub repository (a process known as *cloning*). If a terminal session isn't running, choose **Window, New Terminal** on the menu bar in the IDE. For the

commands to use to run in the terminal session to clone the GitHub repository, see Cloning a Repository on the GitHub Help website. **Note**
To navigate to the main page of the GitHub repository, with the related project open in the AWS CodeStar console, choose **Code** on the console's side navigation bar.

4. Use the IDE's **Environment** window and editor tabs to view, change, and save code. For more information, see The Environment Window and The Editor, Tabs, and Panes in the *AWS Cloud9 User Guide*.

5. Use Git in the IDE's terminal session to push your code changes to the repository and periodically pull code changes from others from the repository. For more information, see Pushing to a Remote and Fetching a remote on the GitHub Help website. For additional Git commands, see Git cheatsheet on the GitHub Help website. **Note**
To keep Git from asking for your GitHub user name and password every time you push or pull code from the repository, you can use a *credential helper*. For more information, see Caching your GitHub password in Git on the GitHub Help website.

Additional Resources

For more information about using AWS Cloud9, see the following in the *AWS Cloud9 User Guide*:

- Tutorial
- Working with Environments
- Working with the IDE
- Samples

Use Eclipse with AWS CodeStar

You can use Eclipse to make code changes and develop software in an AWS CodeStar project. You can edit your AWS CodeStar project code with Eclipse and then commit and push your changes to the source repository for the AWS CodeStar project.

Note

The information in this topic applies only to AWS CodeStar projects that store their source code in AWS CodeCommit. If your AWS CodeStar project stores its source code in GitHub, you can use a tool such as EGit for Eclipse. For more information, see the EGit website and EGit Documentation on the EGit website.

If the AWS CodeStar project stores its source code in AWS CodeCommit, you must install a version of the AWS Toolkit for Eclipse that supports AWS CodeStar. You must also be a member of the AWS CodeStar project team with the owner or contributor role.

To use Eclipse, you'll also need:

- An IAM user that has been added to an AWS CodeStar project as a team member.
- If the AWS CodeStar project stores its source code in AWS CodeCommit, Git credentials (user name and password) for the IAM user.
- Sufficient permissions to install Eclipse and the AWS Toolkit for Eclipse on your local computer.

Topics

- Step 1: Install AWS Toolkit for Eclipse
- Step 2: Import Your AWS CodeStar Project to Eclipse
- Step 3: Edit AWS CodeStar Project Code in Eclipse

Step 1: Install AWS Toolkit for Eclipse

The Toolkit for Eclipse is a software package you can add to Eclipse. It is installed and managed in the same way as other software packages in Eclipse. The AWS CodeStar toolkit is included as part of the Toolkit for Eclipse.

To install the Toolkit for Eclipse with the AWS CodeStar module

1. Install Eclipse on your local computer if you don't have a supported version already installed. Supported versions of Eclipse include Luna, Mars, and Neon.

2. Download and install the Toolkit for Eclipse. For more information, see the AWS Toolkit for Eclipse Getting Started Guide.

3. In Eclipse, choose **Help**, and then choose **Install New Software**.

4. In **Available Software**, choose **Add**.

5. In **Add Repository**, choose **Archive**, browse to the location where you saved the .zip file, and open the file. Leave **Name** blank, and then choose **OK**.

6. In **Available Software**, choose **Select all** to select both **AWS Core Management Tools** and **Developer Tools**, and then choose **Next**.

7. In **Install Details**, choose **Next**.

8. In **Review Licenses**, review the license agreements. If you agree, choose **I accept the terms of the license agreement** and choose **Finish**. Restart Eclipse.

Step 2: Import Your AWS CodeStar Project to Eclipse

After you have installed the Toolkit for Eclipse, you can import AWS CodeStar projects and edit, commit, and push code from the IDE.

Note

You can add multiple AWS CodeStar projects to a single workspace in Eclipse, but if you do, you must update your project credentials when you change from one project to another.

To import an AWS CodeStar project

1. Open the drop-down menu on the AWS toolbar icon and choose **Import AWS CodeStar Project**. Alternatively, choose **File**, and then choose **Import**. In **Select**, expand **AWS**, and then choose ** AWS CodeStar Project**.

   Choose **Next**.

2. In **AWS CodeStar Project Selection**, choose your AWS profile and the region where the AWS CodeStar project is hosted. If you do not have an AWS profile configured with an access key and secret key on your computer, choose **Configure AWS accounts** and follow the instructions.

   In **Select AWS CodeStar project and repository**, choose your AWS CodeStar project from the list. In **Configure Git credentials**, provide the user name and password you generated for access to the project's repository. (If you don't have Git credentials, see Getting Started.) Choose **Next**.

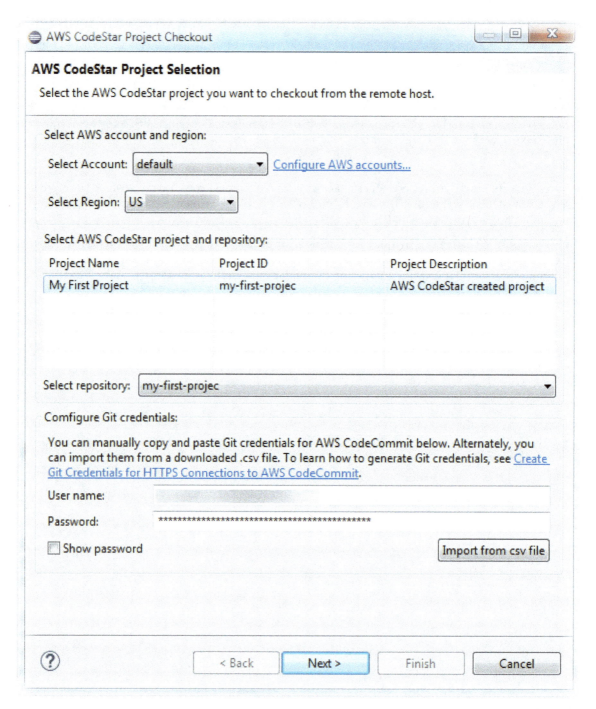

3. All branches of the project's repository are selected by default. If you don't want to import one or more branches, clear the boxes, and then choose **Next**.

4. In **Local Destination**, choose a destination where the import wizard will create the local repo on your computer, and then choose **Finish**.

5. In **Project Explorer**, expand the project tree to browse the files in the AWS CodeStar project.

Step 3: Edit AWS CodeStar Project Code in Eclipse

After you have imported an AWS CodeStar project into an Eclipse workspace, you can edit the code for the project, save your changes, and commit and push your code to the source repository for the project. This is the same process you follow for any Git repository using the EGit plugin for Eclipse. For more information, see the EGit User Guide.

To edit project code and make your first commit to the source repository for an AWS CodeStar project

1. In **Project Explorer**, expand the project tree to browse the files in the AWS CodeStar project.

2. Edit one or more code files and save your changes.

3. When you are ready to commit your changes, open the context menu for that file, choose **Team**, and then choose **Commit**.

   You can skip this step if you have the **Git Staging** window already open in your project view.

4. In the **Git Staging** window, stage your changes by moving modified files into **Staged Changes**. Type a commit message in **Commit Message**, and then choose **Commit and Push**.

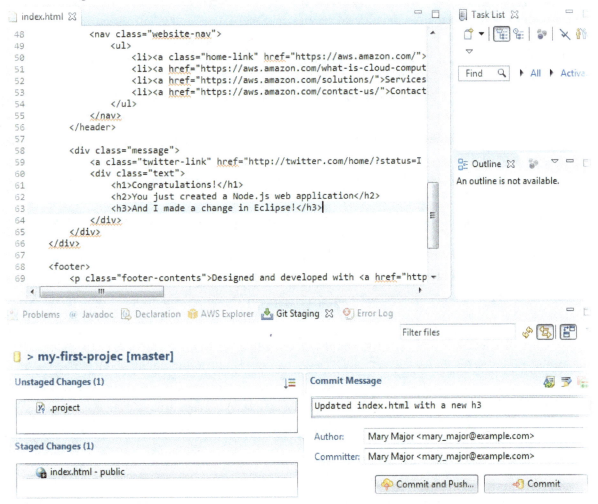

To view the deployment of your code changes, return to the dashboard for your project. For more information, see Step 3: View Your Project.

Use Visual Studio with AWS CodeStar

You can use Visual Studio to make code changes and develop software in an AWS CodeStar project.

Note
The information in this topic applies only to AWS CodeStar projects that store their source code in AWS CodeCommit. If your AWS CodeStar project stores its source code in GitHub, you can use a tool such as the GitHub Extension for Visual Studio. For more information, see the Overview page on the GitHub Extension for Visual Studio website and Getting Started with GitHub for Visual Studio on the GitHub website.

If the AWS CodeStar project stores its source code in AWS CodeCommit, to use Visual Studio to edit code in the source repository for an AWS CodeStar project, you must install a version of the AWS Toolkit for Visual Studio that supports AWS CodeStar. You must be a member of the AWS CodeStar project team with the Owner or Contributor role.

To use Visual Studio, you'll also need:

- An IAM user that has been added to an AWS CodeStar project as a team member.
- If the AWS CodeStar project stores its source code in AWS CodeCommit, AWS credentials for your IAM user, for example your access key and secret key.
- Sufficient permissions to install Visual Studio and the AWS Toolkit for Visual Studio on your local computer.

The Toolkit for Visual Studio is a software package you can add to Visual Studio. It is installed and managed in the same way as other software packages in Visual Studio.

To install the Toolkit for Visual Studio with the AWS CodeStar module and configure access to your project repository

1. Install Visual Studio on your local computer if you don't have a supported version already installed.

2. Download and install the Toolkit for Visual Studio and save the .zip file to a local folder or directory. When prompted on the **Getting Started with the AWS Toolkit for Visual Studio** page, type or import your AWS credentials, and then choose** Save and Close**.

3. In **Visual Studio**, open **Team Explorer**. In **Hosted Service Providers**, find **AWS CodeCommit**, and choose **Connect**.

4. In **Manage Connections**, choose **Clone**. Choose your project's repository and the folder you want to clone the repository into on your local computer, and then choose **OK**.

5. If the AWS CodeStar project stores its source code in AWS CodeCommit, and if prompted to create Git credentials, choose **Yes**. The toolkit will attempt to create credentials on your behalf. Save the credentials file when prompted in a secure location. This is the only opportunity you will have to save these credentials. If the toolkit cannot create credentials on your behalf, or if you chose **No**, you must create and provide your own Git credentials. For more information, see To set up your computer to commit changes (IAM User), or follow the on-screen directions.

6. When you have finished cloning the project, you're ready to start editing your code in Visual Studio and committing and pushing your changes to your project's repository in AWS CodeCommit.

Customize an AWS CodeStar Dashboard

You can customize your project dashboard by adding, removing, and moving tiles. You can also customize the team wiki tile to show information about your project.

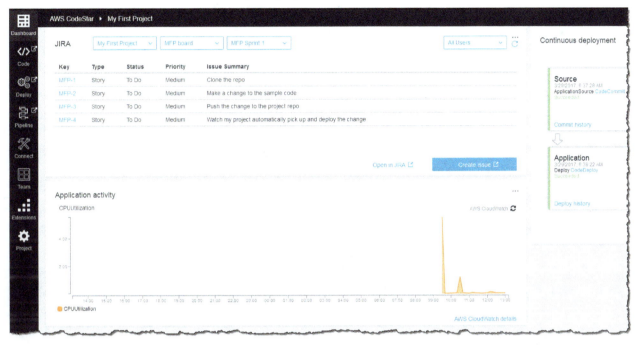

Topics

- Add, Remove, or Move Tiles on Your Dashboard
- Add a Project Extension to Your Dashboard
- Customize the Team Wiki Tile

Add, Remove, or Move Tiles on Your Dashboard

You can change the appearance of your project dashboard by adding tiles, removing tiles, or changing the order and position of tiles on your dashboard.

To change the appearance of your project dashboard, do one or more of the following:

- To add a tile, on the project dashboard, choose **Add tile** and choose the tile from the list. You can only add one of each type of tile.
- To remove a tile, on the project dashboard, choose the ellipsis menu on the tile, and then choose **Remove from dashboard**.
- To change the position of a tile on the dashboard, drag it to the position where you want it to appear.

Add a Project Extension to Your Dashboard

AWS CodeStar includes extensions that add tiles and functionality to your dashboard. For example, you can configure the JIRA extension to add and configure a JIRA tile for your project dashboard.

To add a project extension to your dashboard, on the navigation bar for your project, choose **Extensions**. Then choose **Show on dashboard** next to the extension you want to add.

To set up an extension that is displayed on your dashboard, choose the connect button or command on the extension. Then follow the on-screen instructions to complete setup.

To remove an extension that is displayed on your dashboard, do one of the following:

- Choose the ellipsis menu on the extension you want to remove, and then choose **Remove from Dashboard**.
- On the navigation bar for your project, choose **Extensions**. Then choose **Hide from dashboard** next to the extension you want to remove.

Customize the Team Wiki Tile

Each AWS CodeStar project includes a customizable team wiki tile. You can change the name of this tile as well as its contents. You can use this customizable tile to share links to team resources or highlight code samples. Every project team member can view this tile, but only team members who are assigned a Contributor or Owner role can modify its contents. This tile supports both plain text and CommonMark content, with the following differences:

- You can highlight programming language syntax in code blocks. To do this, specify the language, followed by the code. For example, for JavaScript:

```
1 ```JavaScript
2 var hello = function() {
3   console.log("hello world");
4 }
```

- Inline embedding of images is not supported.

Note
Do not use this tile to store confidential data.

To customize a team wiki tile in a project

1. Open the AWS CodeStar console at https://console.aws.amazon.com/codestar/.

   Choose the project from the list of projects.

2. In the project dashboard, choose the ellipsis button for the project information tile, and then choose **Edit**.

3. In **Markdown Editor**, enter the new tile name in **Title**. In **Markdown content**, add plain text or CommonMark content. For example, you could add a link to your team project wiki or other content.

   Choose **Save**.

For a step-by-step example, see Step 4: Customize the Team Wiki Tile and the Project Dashboard.

66

Change AWS Resources in an AWS CodeStar Project

After you create a project in AWS CodeStar, you can change the default set of AWS resources that AWS CodeStar adds to the project. The following information describes the types of changes AWS CodeStar supports.

Supported Resource Changes

The following table lists the supported and unsupported changes to default AWS resources in an AWS CodeStar project.

Change	Supported?	Notes
Add a stage to AWS Code-Pipeline.	Yes	See Add a Stage to AWS Code-Pipeline.
Change Elastic Beanstalk environment settings.	Yes	See Change AWS Elastic Beanstalk Environment Settings.
Change an AWS Lambda function's code or settings, its related IAM role, or its related API in Amazon API Gateway.	Yes	See Change an AWS Lambda Project.
Add AWS X-Ray support	No	
Switch to a different deployment target (for example, deploy to AWS Elastic Beanstalk instead of AWS CodeDeploy).	No	
Change an IAM role definition.	No	
Add a friendly web endpoint name.	No	
Change the AWS CodeCommit repository name (for an AWS CodeStar project connected to AWS CodeCommit).	No	

Change	Supported?	Notes
Disconnect the GitHub repository (for an AWS CodeStar project connected to GitHub) and then reconnect the repository to that project, or connect any other repository to that project.	No	You can use the AWS Code-Pipeline console (not the AWS CodeStar console) to disconnect and reconnect to GitHub in a pipeline's **Source** stage. However, if you reconnect the **Source** stage to a different GitHub repository, then in the AWS CodeStar dashboard for the project, the information in the **Application endpoints, Commit history**, and **GitHub Issues** tiles might be wrong or out of date. Disconnecting the GitHub repository does not remove that repository's information from the commit history and GitHub issues tiles in the AWS CodeStar dashboard for the project. To remove this information, use the GitHub website to disable access to GitHub from the AWS CodeStar project. To do this, on the GitHub website, revoke access using the **Authorized OAuth Apps** section of the settings page for your GitHub account profile.
Disconnect the AWS Code-Commit repository (for an AWS CodeStar project connected to AWS CodeCommit) and then reconnect the repository to that project, or connect any other repository to that project.	No	
Modify the buildspec.yml file for your project to add a unit test build phase AWS Code-Build runs.	Yes	See Step 7: Add a Unit Test to the Web Service.

Add a Stage to AWS CodePipeline

You can add a new stage to a pipeline that AWS CodeStar creates in a project. For more information, see Edit a Pipeline in AWS CodePipeline in the *AWS CodePipeline User Guide*.

Note

If the new stage depends on any AWS resources that AWS CodeStar did not create, then the pipeline might break. This is because the IAM role that AWS CodeStar created for AWS CodePipeline might not have access to those resources by default.

To attempt to give AWS CodePipeline access to AWS resources that AWS CodeStar did not create, you might want to change the IAM role that AWS CodeStar created. This is not supported because AWS CodeStar might remove your IAM role changes when it performs regular update checks on the project.

Change AWS Elastic Beanstalk Environment Settings

You can change the settings of an Elastic Beanstalk environment that AWS CodeStar creates in a project. For more information, see AWS Elastic Beanstalk Environment Management Console in the *AWS Elastic Beanstalk Developer Guide*.

Change an AWS Lambda Project

You can change the code or settings of a Lambda function, or its related IAM role or API Gateway API, that AWS CodeStar creates in a project. To do this, we recommend you use the AWS Serverless Application Model (AWS SAM) along with the `template.yaml` file in your project's AWS CodeCommit repository. This `template.yaml` file defines your function's name, handler, runtime, related IAM role, and related API in API Gateway. For more information, see How to Create Serverless Applications Using AWS SAM on the GitHub website.

Working with Project Tags in AWS CodeStar

You can associate tags with projects in AWS CodeStar. Tags can help you manage your projects. For example, you could add a tag with a key of `Release` and a value of `Beta` to any project your organization is working on for an upcoming beta release.

Add a Tag to a Project

1. With the project open in the AWS CodeStar console, in the navigation pane, choose **Project**.

2. In the **Tags** area, for **Create new tag**, type the tag's name in the **Key** box. Then type the tag's value in the **Value** box.

3. Choose **Add tag**.

Remove a Tag from a Project

1. With the project open in the AWS CodeStar console, in the navigation pane, choose **Project**.

2. In the **Tags** area, for **Current tags**, find the tag you want to remove.

3. In the **Options** column for that tag, choose **Remove**. **Note**
   You have approximately three seconds to undo the remove operation. To keep the tag, choose **Undo**. Otherwise, the tag is permanently deleted.

Get a List of Tags for a Project

Use the AWS Command Line Interface (AWS CLI) to run the AWS CodeStar `list-tags-for-project` command, specifying the name of the project. For example:

```
1 aws codestar list-tags-for-project --id my-first-projec
```

If successful, a list of tags appears in the output, similar to the following:

```
1 {
2   "tags": {
3     "Release": "Beta"
4   }
5 }
```

Delete an AWS CodeStar Project

If you no longer need a project, you can delete it and its resources so that you do not incur any further charges in AWS. When you delete a project, all team members are removed from that project. Their project roles are removed from their IAM users, but their user profiles in AWS CodeStar are not changed.

Important
Deleting a project in AWS CodeStar cannot be undone. By default all AWS resources for the project are deleted in your AWS account, including:
The AWS CodeCommit repository for the project along with anything stored in that repository. The AWS CodeStar project roles and the associated IAM policies configured for the project and its resources. Any Amazon EC2 instances created for the project. The deployment application and associated resources, such as:
An AWS CodeDeploy application and associated deployment groups. An AWS Lambda function and associated API Gateway APIs. An AWS Elastic Beanstalk application and associated environment. The continuous deployment pipeline for the project in AWS CodePipeline. The AWS CloudFormation stacks associated with the project. Any AWS Cloud9 development environments created with the AWS CodeStar console. All uncommitted code changes in the environments will be lost. To delete all project resources along with the project, select the **Delete associated resources along with AWS CodeStar project** check box. If you clear this option, the project will be deleted in AWS CodeStar, and the project roles that enabled access to those resources will be deleted in IAM, but all other resources will be retained. You might continue to incur charges for these resources in AWS. If you decide you no longer want one or more of these resources, you must manually delete them. For more information about manually deleting resources after a project has been deleted, see Project deletion: An AWS CodeStar project was deleted, but resources still exist.
If you decide to keep resources when deleting a project, as a best practice, copy the list of resources from the project details page before you delete an AWS CodeStar project. This way, you will have a record of all resources that you have kept, even though the project no longer exists.

Topics

- Delete a Project in AWS CodeStar Using the Console
- Delete a Project in AWS CodeStar Using the AWS CLI

Delete a Project in AWS CodeStar Using the Console

Use the AWS CodeStar console to delete a project.

To delete a project in AWS CodeStar

1. Open the AWS CodeStar console at https://console.aws.amazon.com/codestar/.

2. Find the project in the list, and from the ellipsis menu, choose **Delete**.

   Alternatively, open the project, and in the navigation pane, choose **Project**. On the project details page, choose **Delete project**.

3. In the box next to **Type the following project ID to confirm**, type the ID of the project, and then choose **Delete**.

   Deleting a project can take several minutes. After it's deleted, the project no longer appears in the list of projects in the AWS CodeStar console. **Important**
   By default, when you delete a project, all resources listed under **Project resources** are deleted. If you clear the check box, the project resources are retained. For more information, go here.
   If your project uses resources outside of AWS (for example, a GitHub repository or issues in Atlassian JIRA), those resources are not deleted, even if you select the check box.
   Your project cannot be deleted if any AWS CodeStar managed policies have been manually attached to roles that are not IAM users. If you have attached your project's managed policies to a federated user's role, you must detach the policy before you can delete the project. For more information, see Detach an AWS CodeStar Managed Policy from the Federated User's Role.

Delete a Project in AWS CodeStar Using the AWS CLI

You can use the AWS CLI to delete a project in AWS CodeStar.

To delete a project in AWS CodeStar (AWS CLI)

1. At a terminal (Linux, macOS, or Unix) or command prompt (Windows), run the delete-project command, including the name of the project. For example, to delete a project with the ID *my-2nd-project*:

```
1 aws codestar delete-project --id my-2nd-project
```

This command returns output similar to the following:

```
1 {
2     "projectArn":"arn:aws:codestar:us-east-2:111111111111:project/my-2nd-project"
3 }
```

2. Run the list-projects command and verify that the deleted project no longer appears in the list of projects associated with your AWS account.

```
1 aws codestar list-projects
```

Change a Serverless Project to Shift Traffic Between AWS Lambda Function Versions

AWS CodeDeploy supports function version deployments for AWS Lambda functions in your AWS CodeStar serverless projects. An AWS Lambda deployment shifts incoming traffic from an existing Lambda function to an updated Lambda function version. You might want to test an updated Lambda function by deploying a separate version and then rolling back the deployment to the first version if needed.

Use the steps in this section to modify your AWS CodeStar project template and update your CodeStarWorker role's IAM permissions. This task starts an automated response in AWS CloudFormation that creates aliased AWS Lambda functions and then instructs AWS CodeDeploy to shift traffic to an updated environment.

AWS CodeDeploy has three deployment options that allow you to shift traffic to versions of your AWS Lambda function in your application:

- **Canary: **Traffic is shifted in two increments. You can choose from predefined canary options that specify the percentage of traffic shifted to your updated Lambda function version in the first increment and the interval, in minutes, before the remaining traffic is shifted in the second increment.
- **Linear: **Traffic is shifted in equal increments with an equal number of minutes between each increment. You can choose from predefined linear options that specify the percentage of traffic shifted in each incrememnt and the number of minutes between each increment. Traffic is shifted in equal increments with an equal number of minutes between each increment. You can choose from predefined linear options that specify the percentage of traffic shifted in each increment and the number of minutes between each increment.
- **All-at-once: **All traffic is shifted from the original Lambda function to the updated Lambda function version at once.

Deployment Preference Type
Canary10Percent30Minutes
Canary10Percent5Minutes
Canary10Percent10Minutes
Canary10Percent15Minutes
Linear10PercentEvery10Minutes
Linear10PercentEvery1Minute
Linear10PercentEvery2Minutes
Linear10PercentEvery3Minutes
AllAtOnce

For more information about AWS CodeDeploy deployments on an AWS Lambda compute platform, see Deployments on an AWS Lambda Compute Platform.

For more information about AWS SAM, see AWS Serverless Application Model (AWS SAM) on GitHub.

**Prerequisites: **

You can start with an existing serverless project in AWS CodeStar, or you can create a new serverless project in AWS CodeStar and then complete these steps. To create a serverless project, when selecting the template in AWS CodeStar, select any template with the Lambda compute platform.

Topics

Step 1: To modify the SAM template to add AWS Lambda version deployment parameters

1. Open the AWS CodeStar console, at https://console.aws.amazon.com/codestar/.

2. Choose your existing serverless project and then open the **Code** page. In the top level of your repository, note the location of the SAM template named `template.yml` to be modified.

3. Open the `template.yml` file in your IDE or local repository. Add a new `Globals` section by copying this text. The sample text in this tutorial chooses the Canary10Percent5Minutes option.

```
1  Globals:
2    Function:
3      AutoPublishAlias: live
4      DeploymentPreference:
5        Enabled: true
6        Type: Canary10Percent5Minutes
```

This example shows a modified template after the `Globals` section has been added:

```
AWSTemplateFormatVersion: 2010-09-09
Transform:
- AWS::Serverless-2016-10-31
- AWS::CodeStar

Parameters:
  ProjectId:
    Type: String
    Description: CodeStar projectId used to associate new resources to team members

Globals:
  Function:
    AutoPublishAlias: live
    DeploymentPreference:
      Enabled: true
      Type: Canary10Percent5Minutes

Resources:
  HelloWorld:
    Type: AWS::Serverless::Function
    Properties:
      Handler: index.handler
      Runtime: python3.6
      Role:
        Fn::ImportValue:
          !Join ['-', [!Ref 'ProjectId', !Ref 'AWS::Region', 'LambdaTrustRole']]
      Events:
        GetEvent:
```

For more information, see the Globals Section reference guide for serverless application model (SAM) templates.

Step 2: To edit the CloudFormation role to add permissions

1. Sign in to the AWS Management Console and open the AWS CodeStar console, at https://console.aws.amazon.com/codestar/. **Note**
   You must sign in to the AWS Management Console using credentials associated with the IAM user you created or identified in Setting Up AWS CodeStar. This user must have the AWS managed policy named **AWSCodeStarFullAccess** attached.

2. Choose your existing serverless project and then open the Project resources page.

3. Under **Resources**, choose the IAM role created for the CodeStarWorker/AWS CloudFormation role. The role opens in the IAM console. **Note**
   You must complete the following steps with administrator privileges that allow you to add permissions in IAM.

4. On the **Permissions** tab, in **Inline Policies**, in the row for your service role policy, choose **Edit Policy**. Choose the **JSON** tab to edit the policy in JSON format. **Note**
   Your service role has this name: `CodeStarWorkerCloudFormationRolePolicy`.

5. Add the following policy statements in the **JSON** box within the `Statement` element. Replace the *region* and *id* placeholders with your region and account ID.

```
1  {
2    "Action": [
3      "s3:GetObject",
4      "s3:GetObjectVersion",
5      "s3:GetBucketVersioning"
6    ],
7    "Resource": "*",
8    "Effect": "Allow"
9  },
10 {
11   "Action": [
12     "s3:PutObject"
13   ],
14   "Resource": [
15     "arn:aws:s3:::codepipeline*"
16   ],
17   "Effect": "Allow"
18 },
19 {
20   "Action": [
21     "lambda:*"
22   ],
23   "Resource": [
24     "arn:aws:lambda:region:id:function:*"
25   ],
26   "Effect": "Allow"
27 },
28 {
29   "Action": [
30     "apigateway:*"
31   ],
32   "Resource": [
33     "arn:aws:apigateway:region::*"
34   ],
35   "Effect": "Allow"
36 },
37 {
38   "Action": [
39     "iam:GetRole",
40     "iam:CreateRole",
41     "iam:DeleteRole",
42     "iam:PutRolePolicy"
43   ],
44   "Resource": [
45     "arn:aws:iam::id:role/*"
46   ],
47   "Effect": "Allow"
48 },
49 {
50   "Action": [
51     "iam:AttachRolePolicy",
52     "iam:DeleteRolePolicy",
```

```
53        "iam:DetachRolePolicy"
54      ],
55      "Resource": [
56        "arn:aws:iam::id:role/*"
57      ],
58      "Effect": "Allow"
59    },
60    {
61      "Action": [
62        "iam:PassRole"
63      ],
64      "Resource": [
65        "*"
66      ],
67      "Effect": "Allow"
68    },
69    {
70      "Action": [
71        "codedeploy:CreateApplication",
72        "codedeploy:DeleteApplication",
73        "codedeploy:RegisterApplicationRevision"
74      ],
75      "Resource": [
76        "arn:aws:codedeploy:region:id:application:*"
77      ],
78      "Effect": "Allow"
79    },
80    {
81      "Action": [
82        "codedeploy:CreateDeploymentGroup",
83        "codedeploy:CreateDeployment",
84        "codedeploy:DeleteDeploymentGroup",
85        "codedeploy:GetDeployment"
86      ],
87      "Resource": [
88        "arn:aws:codedeploy:region:id:deploymentgroup:*"
89      ],
90      "Effect": "Allow"
91    },
92    {
93      "Action": [
94        "codedeploy:GetDeploymentConfig"
95      ],
96      "Resource": [
97        "arn:aws:codedeploy:region:id:deploymentconfig:*"
98      ],
99      "Effect": "Allow"
100   }
```

6. Choose **Review policy** to ensure the policy contains no errors. When the policy is error-free, choose **Save changes**.

Step 3: To commit and push your template change to start the AWS Lambda version shift

1. Commit and push the changes in the template.yml file that you saved in Step 1. **Note**
This will start your pipeline. If you commit the changes before updating IAM permissions, your pipeline

starts and CloudFormation stack creation encounters errors, which will roll back the stack creation. If this happens, restart your pipeline after permissions have been corrected.

2. When the pipeline for your project starts the deployment stage, the AWS CloudFormation stack creation starts. You can select the AWS CloudFormation stage in your pipeline on your AWS CodeStar dashboard to see the stack creation notice when deployment is started.

   During stack creation, AWS CloudFormation automatically updates the project resources as follows:

   - AWS CloudFormation processes the template.yml file by creating aliased Lambda functions, event hooks, and resources.
   - AWS CloudFormation calls Lambda to create the new version of the function.
   - AWS CloudFormation creates an AppSpec file and calls AWS CodeDeploy to shift the traffic.

   For more information on publishing aliased Lambda functions in the serverless application model (SAM), see the AWS Serverless Application Model (SAM) template reference. For more information about event hooks and resources in the AWS CodeDeploy AppSpec file, see AppSpec 'resources' Section (AWS Lambda Deployments Only) and AppSpec 'hooks' Section for an AWS Lambda Deployment.

3. After successful completion of your pipeline, the resources are created in your AWS CloudFormation stack. In the **Project Resources ** list on the **Project** page in AWS CodeStar, view the AWS CodeDeploy application, the AWS CodeDeploy deployment group, and the AWS CodeDeploy service role resources created for your project.

4. Make a change in your Lambda function in your repository to create a new version. The new deployment starts and shifts traffic according to the deployment type indicated in the SAM template. You can view the status of the deployment. In the **Project Resources ** list on the **Project** page in AWS CodeStar, choose the link to the AWS CodeDeploy deployment to view the status of the traffic shifting to the new

version.

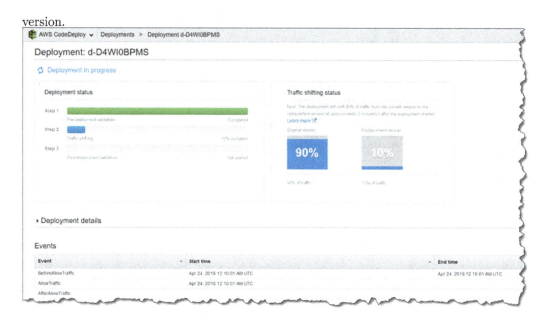

5. Choose the link to the AWS CodeDeploy deployment group to view details on each revision under **Revisions**.

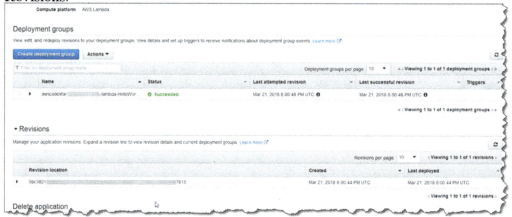

6. In your local working directory, you can make changes to your AWS Lambda function and commit the change to your project repository. AWS CloudFormation supports AWS CodeDeploy in managing the next revision in the same way. For more information on redeploying, stopping, or rolling back a Lambda deployment, see Deployments on an AWS Lambda Compute Platform.

Working with AWS CodeStar Teams

After you create a development project, you'll want to grant access to others so you can work together. In AWS CodeStar, each project has a *project team*. A user can belong to multiple AWS CodeStar projects and have different AWS CodeStar roles (and thus, different permissions) in each. In the AWS CodeStar console, users see all projects associated with your AWS account, but they will only be able to view and work on those projects in which they are team members.

Team members can choose a friendly name for themselves. They can also add an email address so other team members can contact them. Team members who are not owners cannot change their AWS CodeStar role for the project.

Each project in AWS CodeStar has three roles:

Roles and Permissions in an AWS CodeStar Project

Role Name	View Project Dashboard and Status	Add/Remove/Access Project Resources	Add/Remove Team Members	Delete Project
Owner	x	x	x	x
Contributor	x	x		
Viewer	x			

- **Owner**: Can add and remove other team members, contribute code to a project repository if the code is stored in AWS CodeCommit, grant or deny other team members remote access to any Amazon EC2 instances running Linux associated with the project, configure the project dashboard, and delete the project.
- **Contributor**: Can add and remove dashboard resources such as a JIRA tile, contribute code to the project repository if the code is stored in AWS CodeCommit, and interact fully with the dashboard. Cannot add or remove team members, grant or deny remote access to resources, or delete the project. This is the role you should choose for most team members.
- **Viewer**: Can view the project dashboard, the code if is stored in AWS CodeCommit, and, on the dashboard tiles, the state of the project and its resources.

Important
If your project uses resources outside of AWS, for example a GitHub repository or issues in Atlassian JIRA, access to those resources are controlled by the resource provider, not AWS CodeStar. For more information, see the resource provider's documentation.
Anyone who has access to an AWS CodeStar project may be able to use the AWS CodeStar console to access resources that are outside of AWS but are related to that project.
AWS CodeStar does not automatically allow project team members to participate in any related AWS Cloud9 development environments for a project. To allow a team member to participate in a shared environment, see Share an AWS Cloud9 Environment with a Project Team Member.

An IAM policy is associated with each project role. This policy is customized for your project to reflect its resources. For more information about these policies, see AWS CodeStar Access Permissions Reference.

The following diagram shows the relationship between each role and an AWS CodeStar project.

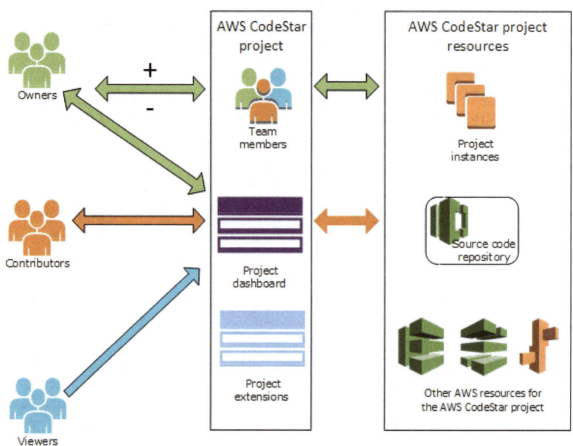

Topics

- Add Team Members to an AWS CodeStar Project
- Manage Permissions for AWS CodeStar Team Members
- Remove Team Members from an AWS CodeStar Project

Add Team Members to an AWS CodeStar Project

If you have the Owner role in an AWS CodeStar project or have the **AWSCodeStarFullAccess** policy applied to your IAM user, you can add other IAM users to the project team. This is a simple process that applies an AWS CodeStar role (Owner, Contributor, and Viewer) to the user. These roles are per-project and customized. For example, a Contributor team member in ProjectA might have permissions to resources that are different from those of a Contributor team member in ProjectB. A team member can have only one role in a project. After you've added a team member, he or she can interact immediately with your project at the level defined by the role.

Benefits of AWS CodeStar roles and team membership include:

- You do not have to manually configure permissions in IAM for your team members.
- You can easily change a team member's level of access to a project.
- Users can access project dashboards in the AWS CodeStar console only if they are team members.
- User access to a project is defined by the role in that project. A user can have a different role in another project.

For more information about teams and AWS CodeStar roles, see Working with AWS CodeStar Teams and Working with Your AWS CodeStar User Profile .

To add a team member to a project, you must either have the AWS CodeStar Owner role for that project or have the **AWSCodeStarFullAccess** policy.

Important
Adding a team member does not affect that team member's access to any resources that are outside of AWS, for example a GitHub repository or issues in Atlassian JIRA. Those access permissions are controlled by the resource provider, not AWS CodeStar. For more information, consult the resource provider's documentation.
Anyone who has access to an AWS CodeStar project may be able to use the AWS CodeStar console to access resources that are outside of AWS but are related to that project.
Adding a team member to a project does not automatically allow that member to participate in any related AWS Cloud9 development environments for the project. To allow a team member to participate in a shared environment, see Share an AWS Cloud9 Environment with a Project Team Member.
Granting federated user access to a project involves manually attaching the AWS CodeStar Owner, Contributor, or Viewer managed policy to the role assumed by the federated user. For more information, see Federated User Access to AWS CodeStar.

Topics

- Add a Team Member Using the AWS CodeStar Console
- Add and View Team Members Using the AWS CLI

Add a Team Member Using the AWS CodeStar Console

You can add a team member to your project in the AWS CodeStar console. If an IAM user already exists for the person you want to add, you can add the IAM user directly. If the person does not yet have an IAM user, you can create an IAM user for that person as part of adding them to your project.

To add a team member to an AWS CodeStar project (console)

1. Open the AWS CodeStar console at https://console.aws.amazon.com/codestar/.

   Choose the project.

2. In the navigation bar for the project, choose **Team**.

3. On the **Team members** page, choose **Add team member**.

4. In **Choose user**, do one of the following:

- If an IAM user already exists for the person you want to add, choose the IAM user name from the list. **Note**
  Users who have already been added to another AWS CodeStar project will appear in the **AWS CodeStar users from other projects** list.

  On the **Add team member** tab, in **Project role**, choose the AWS CodeStar role (Owner, Contributor, or Viewer) for this user. This is an AWS CodeStar project-level role that can only be changed by an owner of the project. When applied to an IAM user, the role provides all appropriate permissions required to access AWS CodeStar project resources. It applies policies required for creating and managing Git credentials for code stored in AWS CodeCommit in IAM or uploading Amazon EC2 SSH keys for the user in IAM. **Important**
  You cannot provide or change the display name or email information for an IAM user unless you are signed in to the console as that user. For more information, see Manage Display Information for Your AWS CodeStar User Profile .

  Choose **Add**.

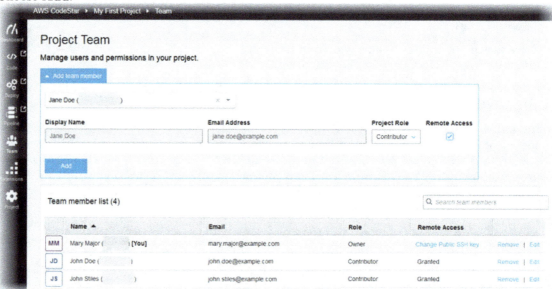

- If an IAM user does not exist for the person you want to add to the project, choose **Create new IAM user**. Fill in the IAM user name, AWS CodeStar display name, email address, and project role you want to apply to this new user, and choose **Create**.

Create IAM user ✖

Create an IAM user to add to your project.

IAM user name

DemoUser

Display Name

John Doe

Email

john.doe@example.com

Project role

Viewer ⌄

Remote access

☐

Cancel   Create

You will be redirected to the IAM console to confirm user creation. Choose **Create user**, save the password information for that new user, and then choose **Close** to return to the AWS CodeStar console. The user will be automatically added to the project with the role you chose. **Note** For ease of management, at least one user should have the **Owner** role for the project.

5. Send the new team member the following information:

- Connection information for your AWS CodeStar project.
- If the source code is stored in AWS CodeCommit, Instructions for setting up access with Git credentials to the AWS CodeCommit repository from their local computers.
- Information about how the user can manage their display name, email address, and public Amazon EC2 SSH key, as described in Working with Your AWS CodeStar User Profile .
- One-time password and connection information, if the user is new to AWS and you created an IAM user for that person. The password will expire the first time the user logs on. The user must choose a new password.

Add and View Team Members Using the AWS CLI

You can add team members to your project team using the AWS CLI. You can also view information about all of the team members in your project.

To add a team member (AWS CLI)

1. Open a terminal or command window.

2. Run the associate-team-member command, including the `--project-id`, `-user-arn`, and `--project-role` parameters to add a team member to your project with an associated role. You can also specify whether the user has remote access to project instances by including the `--remote-access-allowed` or `--no-remote-access-allowed` parameters. For example:

```
1 aws codestar associate-team-member --project-id my-first-projec --user-arn arn:aws:iam
      :111111111111:user/Jane_Doe --project-role Contributor --remote-access-allowed
```

This command returns no output.

To view all team members (AWS CLI)

1. Open a terminal or command window.

2. Run the list-team-members command, including the `--project-id`. For example:

```
1 aws codestar list-team-members --project-id my-first-projec
```

This command returns output similar to the following:

```
1 {
2     "teamMembers":[
3       {"projectRole":"Owner","remoteAccessAllowed":true,"userArn":"arn:aws:iam
            ::111111111111:user/Mary_Major"},
4       {"projectRole":"Contributor","remoteAccessAllowed":true,"userArn":"arn:aws:iam
            ::111111111111:user/Jane_Doe"},
5       {"projectRole":"Contributor","remoteAccessAllowed":true,"userArn":"arn:aws:iam
            ::111111111111:user/John_Doe"},
6       {"projectRole":"Viewer","remoteAccessAllowed":false,"userArn":"arn:aws:iam
            ::111111111111:user/John_Stiles"}
7     ]
8 }
```

Manage Permissions for AWS CodeStar Team Members

You change permissions for team members by changing their AWS CodeStar role. Each team member can be assigned to only one role in an AWS CodeStar project, but many users can be assigned to the same role.

Important
To change a role for a team member, you must either have the AWS CodeStar Owner role for that project or have the **AWSCodeStarFullAccess** policy applied.
Changing a team member's permissions does not affect that team member's access to any resources that are outside of AWS, for example a GitHub repository or issues in Atlassian JIRA. Those access permissions are controlled by the resource provider, not AWS CodeStar. For more information, consult the resource provider's documentation.
Anyone who has access to an AWS CodeStar project may be able to use the AWS CodeStar console to access resources that are outside of AWS but are related to that project.
Changing a team member's role for a project does not automatically allow or prevent that member from participating in any AWS Cloud9 development environments for the project. To allow or prevent a team member from participating in a shared environment, see Share an AWS Cloud9 Environment with a Project Team Member.

You can also grant permissions for users to remotely access any Amazon EC2 instances running Linux associated with the project. After you grant this permission, the user must upload an SSH public key that will be associated with their AWS CodeStar user profile across all team projects. To successfully connect to the Linux instances associated with the project, the user must have SSH configured and the private key on the local computer.

Topics

- Manage Team Permissions Using the AWS CodeStar Console
- Manage Team Permissions Using the AWS CLI

Manage Team Permissions Using the AWS CodeStar Console

You can manage the roles of team members in the AWS CodeStar console. You can also manage whether team members have remote access to the Amazon EC2 instances associated with your project.

To change the role of a team member (console)

1. Open the AWS CodeStar console at https://console.aws.amazon.com/codestar/.

   Choose the project.

2. In the navigation bar for the project, choose **Team**.

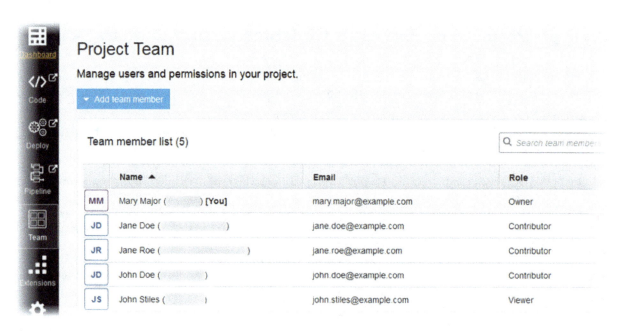

3. On the **Team members** page, find the name of the team member, and then choose **Edit**.

4. In **Role**, choose the AWS CodeStar role (Owner, Contributor, or Viewer) you want to apply to this user.

   For more information about AWS CodeStar roles and their permissions, see Working with AWS CodeStar Teams.

   Choose **Save**.

To grant a team member remote access permissions to Amazon EC2 instances (console)

1. Open the AWS CodeStar console at https://console.aws.amazon.com/codestar/.

   Choose the project.

2. In the navigation bar for the project, choose **Team**.

3. On the **Project team** page, find the name of the team member, and then choose **Edit**.

4. Select the **Allow SSH access to project instances** check box, and then choose **Save**.

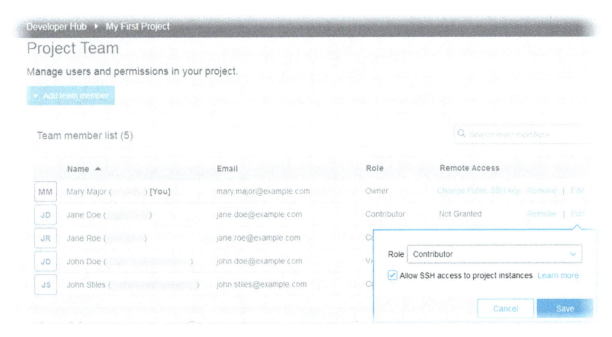

5. (Optional) Notify the team members that they should upload an SSH public key for their AWS CodeStar users, if they have not already done so. For more information, see Add a Public Key to Your AWS CodeStar User Profile .

Manage Team Permissions Using the AWS CLI

You can use the AWS CLI to manage the project role assigned to a team member. You can use the same AWS CLI commands to manage whether that team member has remote access to Amazon EC2 instances associated with your project.

To manage the permissions for a team member (AWS CLI)

1. Open a terminal or command window.

2. Run the update-team-member command, including the `--project-id`, `-user-arn`, and `--project-role` parameters to add a team member to your project with an associated role. You can also specify whether the user has remote access to project instances by including the `--remote-access-allowed` or `--no-remote-access-allowed` parameters. For example, to update the project role of an IAM user named John_Doe and change his permissions to those of a Viewer with no remote access to project Amazon EC2 instances:

```
1 aws codestar update-team-member --project-id my-first-projec --user-arn arn:aws:iam
      :111111111111:user/John_Doe --project-role Viewer --no-remote-access-allowed
```

This command returns output similar to the following:

```
1 {
2   "projectRole":"Viewer",
3   "remoteAccessAllowed":false,
4   "userArn":"arn:aws:iam::111111111111:user/John_Doe"
5 }
```

Remove Team Members from an AWS CodeStar Project

After you remove from an AWS CodeStar project, the user will still appear in the commit history for the project repository, but will no longer have access to the AWS CodeCommit repository or any other project resources, such as the project pipeline. (The exception to this rule is an IAM user who has other policies applied that grant access to those resources.) The user will not be able to access the project dashboard, and the project will no longer appear in the list of projects that user sees on the AWS CodeStar dashboard.

Important

Although removing a team member from a project will deny remote access to project Amazon EC2 instances, it will not close any of the user's active SSH sessions.

Removing a team member does not affect that team member's access to any resources that are outside of AWS, for example a GitHub repository or issues in Atlassian JIRA. Those access permissions are controlled by the resource provider, not AWS CodeStar. For more information, consult the resource provider's documentation.

Removing a team member from a project does not automatically delete that team member's related AWS Cloud9 development environments or prevent that member from participating in any related AWS Cloud9 development environments they have been invited to. To delete a development environment, see Delete an AWS Cloud9 Environment from a Project. To prevent a team member from participating in a shared environment, see Share an AWS Cloud9 Environment with a Project Team Member.

To remove a team member from a project, you must have the AWS CodeStar Owner role for that project or have the **AWSCodeStarFullAccess** policy applied to your account.

Topics

- Remove Team Members Using the Console
- Remove Team Members Using the AWS CLI

Remove Team Members Using the Console

You can remove team members from your project team using the AWS CodeStar console.

To remove a team member from a project

1. Open the AWS CodeStar console at https://console.aws.amazon.com/codestar/.

   Choose the project.

2. In the navigation bar for the project, choose **Team**.

3. On the **Team members** page, find the name of the team member you want to remove, and then choose **Remove**.

Remove Team Members Using the AWS CLI

You can remove team members from your project team using the AWS CLI.

To remove a team member (AWS CLI)

1. Open a terminal or command window.

2. Run the disassociate-team-member command, including the `--project-id` and `-user-arn` parameters to remove a team member from your project. For example:

```
1 aws codestar disassociate-team-member --project-id my-first-projec --user-arn arn:aws:iam
    :111111111111:user/John_Doe
```

   This command returns output similar to the following:

```json
{
    "projectId": "my-first-projec",
    "userArn": "arn:aws:iam::111111111111:user/John_Doe"
}
```

Working with Your AWS CodeStar User Profile

Your AWS CodeStar user profile is associated with your IAM user. This profile contains a display name and email address that is used in all AWS CodeStar projects you belong to. You can upload an SSH public key that will be associated with your profile. This public key is part of the SSH public/private key pair you use when you connect to Amazon EC2 instances associated with AWS CodeStar projects you belong to.

Note
The information in these topics covers only your AWS CodeStar user profile. If your project uses resources outside of AWS, for example a GitHub repository or issues in Atlassian JIRA, those resource providers may use separate user profiles, which may have different settings. For more information, see the resource provider's documentation.

Topics

- Manage Display Information for Your AWS CodeStar User Profile
- Add a Public Key to Your AWS CodeStar User Profile

Manage Display Information for Your AWS CodeStar User Profile

You can change your display name and email information in AWS CodeStar. This information is part of your AWS CodeStar user profile, which is not project-specific, but instead displays in every project you belong to within an AWS region. Because this information is associated with your IAM user, it will be applied across the AWS CodeStar projects you belong to in that region. If you belong to projects in more than one AWS region, you will have a separate user profile in each region.

You can only manage your own user profile in the AWS CodeStar console. If you have the `AWSCodeStarFullAccess` policy, you can view and manage other profiles using the AWS CLI.

Note
The information in this topic covers only your AWS CodeStar user profile. If your project uses resources outside of AWS, for example a GitHub repository or issues in Atlassian JIRA, those resource providers may use separate user profiles, which may have different settings. For more information, see the resource provider's documentation.

Topics

- Manage Your User Profile Using the AWS CodeStar Console
- Manage User Profiles Using the AWS CLI

Manage Your User Profile Using the AWS CodeStar Console

You can manage your user profile in the AWS CodeStar console by navigating to any project where you are a team member and changing your profile information. Because user profiles are user-specific and not project-specific, your user profile changes will appear in every project where you are a team member within an AWS region.

Important
To change the display information for a user in the console, you must be signed in as that IAM user. No other user, even those with AWS CodeStar Owner role for a project or with the **AWSCodeStarFullAccess** policy applied, can change your display information in the console.

To change your display information in all projects within an AWS region (console)

1. Open the AWS CodeStar console at https://console.aws.amazon.com/codestar/.

   Choose a project where you are a team member.

2. In the navigation bar for the project, choose **Team**.

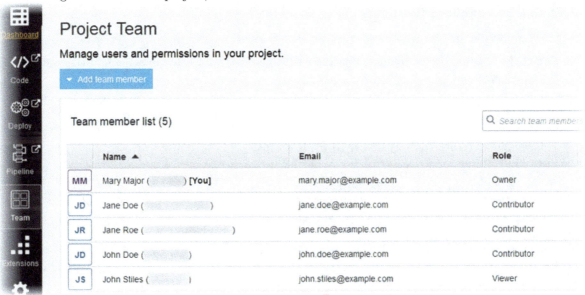

3. On the **Team members** page, find the name of your IAM user (the team member that has your IAM name in parentheses, and has [**You**] in brackets next to the display name), and then choose **Edit**.

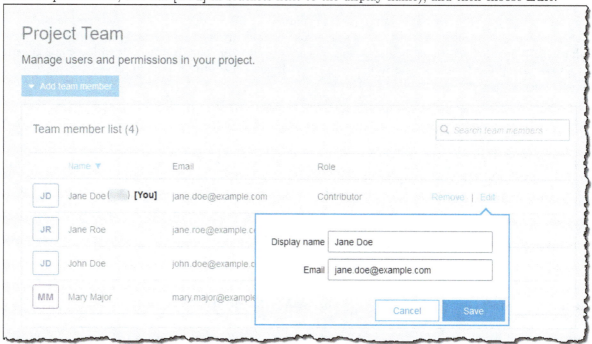

4. Edit the display name, the email address, or both, and then choose **Save. Note**
   Both a display name and an email address are required. For more information, see Limits in AWS CodeStar.

Manage User Profiles Using the AWS CLI

You can use the AWS CLI to create and manage your user profile in AWS CodeStar. You can also use the AWS CLI to view your user profile information, and to view all user profiles configured for your AWS account in an AWS region.

Make sure that your AWS profile is configured for the region where you want to create, manage, or view user profiles, as user profiles are region-specific.

To create a user profile (AWS CLI)

1. Open a terminal or command window.

2. Run the create-user-profile command, including the `user-arn`, `display-name`, and `email-address` parameters. For example:

```
1 aws codestar create-user-profile --user-arn arn:aws:iam:111111111111:user/John_Stiles --
     display-name "John Stiles" --email-address "john_stiles@example.com"
```

This command returns output similar to the following:

```
1 {
2  "createdTimestamp":1.491439687681E9,"
3  displayName":"John Stiles",
4  "emailAddress":"john.stiles@example.com",
5  "lastModifiedTimestamp":1.491439687681E9,
6  "userArn":"arn:aws:iam::111111111111:user/Jane_Doe"
7 }
```

To view your display information (AWS CLI)

1. Open a terminal or command window.

2. Run the describe-user-profile command, including the **user-arn** parameter. For example:

```
1 aws codestar describe-user-profile --user-arn arn:aws:iam:111111111111:user/Mary_Major
```

This command returns output similar to the following:

```
1 {
2   "createdTimestamp":1.490634364532E9,
3   "displayName":"Mary Major",
4   "emailAddress":"mary.major@example.com",
5   "lastModifiedTimestamp":1.491001935261E9,
6   "sshPublicKey":"EXAMPLE=",
7   "userArn":"arn:aws:iam::111111111111:user/Mary_Major"
8 }
```

To change your display information (AWS CLI)

1. Open a terminal or command window.

2. Run the update-user-profile command, including the **user-arn** parameter and the profile parameters you want to change, such as, **display-name** or **email-address** parameters. For example, if a user with the display name "Jane Doe" wanted to change her display name to "Jane Mary Doe":

```
1 aws codestar update-user-profile --user-arn arn:aws:iam:111111111111:user/Jane_Doe --
    display-name "Jane Mary Doe"
```

This command returns output similar to the following:

```
1 {
2   "createdTimestamp":1.491439687681E9,
3   "displayName":"Jane Mary Doe",
4   "emailAddress":"jane.doe@example.com",
5   "lastModifiedTimestamp":1.491442730598E9,
6   "sshPublicKey":"EXAMPLE1",
7   "userArn":"arn:aws:iam::111111111111:user/Jane_Doe"
8 }
```

To list all user profiles in an AWS region in your AWS account (AWS CLI)

1. Open a terminal or command window.

2. Run the aws codestar list-user-profiles command. For example:

```
1 aws codestar list-user-profiles
```

This command returns output similar to the following:

```
1 {
2   "userProfiles":[
3   {
4       "displayName":"Jane Doe",
5       "emailAddress":"jane.doe@example.com",
6       "sshPublicKey":"EXAMPLE1",
7       "userArn":"arn:aws:iam::111111111111:user/Jane_Doe"
8   },
9   {
10      "displayName":"John Doe",
11      "emailAddress":"john.doe@example.com",
```

```
12      "sshPublicKey":"EXAMPLE2",
13      "userArn":"arn:aws:iam::111111111111:user/John_Doe"
14  },
15  {
16      "displayName":"Mary Major",
17      "emailAddress":"mary.major@example.com",
18      "sshPublicKey":"EXAMPLE=",
19      "userArn":"arn:aws:iam::111111111111:user/Mary_Major"
20  },
21  {
22      "displayName":"John Stiles",
23      "emailAddress":"john.stiles@example.com",
24      "sshPublicKey":"",
25      "userArn":"arn:aws:iam::111111111111:user/John_Stiles"
26  }
27  ]
28  }
```

Add a Public Key to Your AWS CodeStar User Profile

You can upload a public SSH key as part of the public/private key pair you create and manage. You use this SSH public/private key pair to access Amazon EC2 instances running Linux. If a project owner has granted you remote access permission, you can access only those instances associated with the project where you were granted access.

Important
An AWS CodeStar project owner can grant project owners, contributors, and viewers SSH access to Amazon EC2 instances for the project. However, only the individual owner, contributor, or viewer can set their own SSH key. To do this, they must be signed in as the individual owner, contributor, or viewer.
AWS CodeStar does not manage SSH keys for AWS Cloud9 environments.

Topics

- Manage Your Public Key Using the AWS CodeStar Console
- Manage Your Public Key Using the AWS CLI
- Connect to Amazon EC2 Instance with Your Private Key

Manage Your Public Key Using the AWS CodeStar Console

Although you cannot generate a public-private key pair in the console, you can create one locally and then add or manage it as part of your user profile through the AWS CodeStar console.

To manage your public SSH key (console)

1. From a terminal or Bash emulator window, run the ssh-keygen command to generate an SSH public/private key pair on your local computer. You can generate a key in any format allowed by Amazon EC2. For information about acceptable formats, see Importing Your Own Public Key to Amazon EC2. Ideally, generate a key that is SSH-2 RSA, in OpenSSH format, and contain 2048 bits. The public key is stored in a file with the .pub extension.

2. Open the AWS CodeStar console at https://console.aws.amazon.com/codestar/.

   Choose a project where you are a team member.

3. In the navigation bar for the project, choose **Team**.

4. On the **Team members** page, find the name of your IAM user (the team member that has your IAM name in parentheses, and has [**You**] in brackets next to the display name), and then choose **Add Public SSH key**.

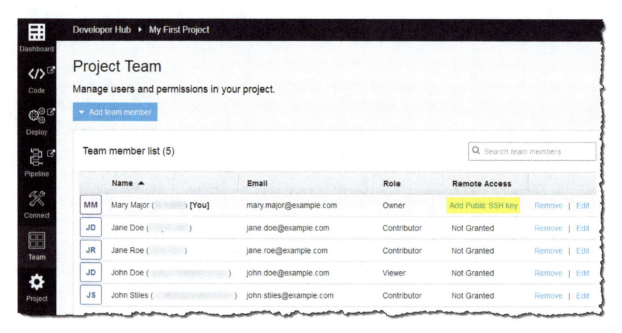

5. In **Manage your public SSH key**, paste the public key, and then choose **Save**.

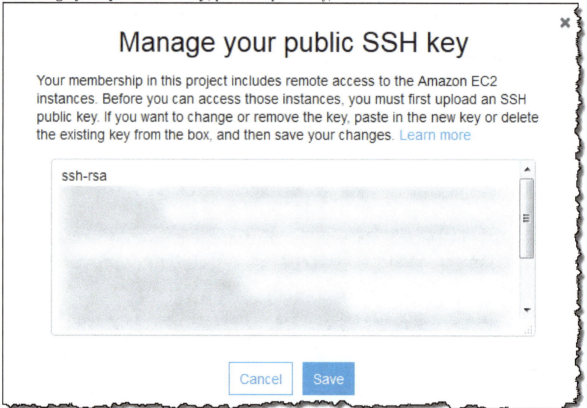

Note

You can change your public key by deleting the old key in this field and pasting in a new one. Similarly, you can delete a public key by deleting the contents of this field and then choosing **Save**.

When you change or delete a public key you are changing your user profile. It is not a per-project change. Because your key is associated with your profile, it will change (or be deleted) in all projects where you have been granted remote access.

Deleting your public key removes your access to Amazon EC2 instances running Linux in all projects where you were granted remote access. However, it does not close any open SSH sessions using that key. Make sure you close any open sessions.

Manage Your Public Key Using the AWS CLI

You can manage your SSH public key as part of your user profile using the AWS CLI. t

To manage your public key (AWS CLI)

1. From a terminal or Bash emulator window, run the ssh-keygen command to generate an SSH public/private key pair on your local computer. You can generate a key in any format allowed by Amazon EC2. For information about acceptable formats, see Importing Your Own Public Key to Amazon EC2. Ideally, generate a key that is SSH-2 RSA, in OpenSSH format, and contain 2048 bits. The public key is stored in a file with the .pub extension.

2. Run the update-user-profile command with the `--ssh-public-key` parameter to add or change your SSH public key in your AWS CodeStar user profile. For example:

```
1 aws codestar update-user-profile --user-arn arn:aws:iam:111111111111:user/Jane_Doe --ssh-
    key-id EXAMPLE1
```

This command returns output similar to the following:

```
1 {
2   "createdTimestamp":1.491439687681E9,
3   "displayName":"Jane Doe",
4   "emailAddress":"jane.doe@example.com",
5   "lastModifiedTimestamp":1.491442730598E9,
6   "sshPublicKey":"EXAMPLE1",
7   "userArn":"arn:aws:iam::111111111111:user/Jane_Doe"
8 }
```

Connect to Amazon EC2 Instance with Your Private Key

Make sure you have already created an Amazon EC2 key pair. Then add your key pair's public key to your user profile in AWS CodeStar. To create a key pair, see Step 4: Create an Amazon EC2 Key Pair for AWS CodeStar Projects in *Setting Up*. To add your key pair's public key to your user profile, see the instructions earlier in this topic.

To connect to an Amazon EC2 instance running Linux by using your key pair's private key

1. With your project open in the AWS CodeStar console, in the navigation pane, choose **Project**.

2. In **Project Resources**, for the row where **Type** is **Amazon EC2** and **Name** starts with **instance**, choose the **ARN** link.

3. When the Amazon EC2 console displays with the instance details, choose **Connect**.

4. Follow the instructions in the **Connect To Your Instance** dialog.

   For the username, use **ubuntu** for projects based on the ASP.NET Core project template, as those instances use Ubuntu. For all other projects, use **ec2-user** for the username, as those instances use Amazon Linux. If you use the wrong username, you will not be able to connect to the instance.

For more information, see the following resources in the *Amazon EC2 User Guide for Linux Instances*.

- Connecting to Your Linux Instance Using SSH
- Connecting to Your Linux Instance from Windows Using PuTTY
- Connecting to Your Linux Instance Using MindTerm

AWS CodeStar Access Permissions Reference

You can use AWS CodeStar as an IAM user, a federated user, the root user, or an assumed role. All user types with the appropriate permissions can manage project permissions to their AWS resources, but AWS CodeStar manages project permissions automatically for IAM users. IAM policies and roles grant permissions and access to that user based on the project role. You can use the IAM console to create other policies that assign AWS CodeStar and other permissions to an IAM user.

For example, you might want to allow a user to view but not change an AWS CodeStar project. In this case, you add the IAM user to an AWS CodeStar project with the Viewer role. Every AWS CodeStar project has a set of policies that help you control access to the project. In addition, you can control which users have access to AWS CodeStar.

In the Setting Up AWS CodeStar instructions, you attached a policy named AWSCodeStarFullAccess to your IAM user. This policy allows full access to AWS CodeStar. That policy statement looks similar to this:

```
1  {
2    "Version": "2012-10-17",
3    "Statement": [
4      {
5        "Sid": "CodeStarEC2",
6        "Effect": "Allow",
7        "Action": [
8          "codestar:*",
9          "ec2:DescribeKeyPairs",
10         "ec2:DescribeVpcs",
11         "ec2:DescribeSubnets"
12       ],
13       "Resource": "*"
14     },
15     {
16       "Sid": "CodeStarCF",
17       "Effect": "Allow",
18       "Action": [
19         "cloudformation:DescribeStack*",
20         "cloudformation:GetTemplateSummary"
21       ],
22       "Resource": [
23         "arn:aws:cloudformation:*:*:stack/awscodestar-*"
24       ]
25     }
26   ]
27 }
```

This policy statement allows the user to perform all available actions in AWS CodeStar with all available AWS CodeStar resources associated with the AWS account. This includes creating and deleting projects. You might not want to give all users this much access. Instead, you can add project-level permissions using project roles managed by AWS CodeStar. The roles grant specific levels of access to AWS CodeStar projects and are named as follows:

- Owner
- Contributor
- Viewer

AWS CodeStar access is handled differently for IAM users and federated users. Only IAM users can be added to teams. To grant IAM users permissions to projects, you add the user to the project role by adding them to the team. To grant federated users permissions to projects, you manually attach the AWS CodeStar project role's managed policy to the federated user's role. This table summarizes the tools available for each type of access.

Permissions feature	IAM user	Federated user	Root user
SSH key management for remote access for EC2 and Elastic Beanstalk projects	✓		
AWS CodeCommit SSH access	✓		
IAM user permissions managed by AWS CodeStar	✓		
Project permissions managed manually		✓	✓
Users can be added to project as team members	✓		

Topics

- AWS CodeStar Project-Level Policies and Permissions
- IAM User Access to AWS CodeStar
- Federated User Access to AWS CodeStar
- AWS CodeStar Service Role Policy and Permissions
- Action and Resource Syntax

AWS CodeStar Project-Level Policies and Permissions

There are three roles in AWS CodeStar projects: Owner, Contributor, and Viewer. Each role is specific to a project and defined by an IAM managed policy, where *project-id* is the ID of the AWS CodeStar project (for example, *my-first-projec*):

- CodeStar_*project-id*_Owner
- CodeStar_*project-id*_Contributor
- CodeStar_*project-id*_Viewer

Important
These policies are subject to change by AWS CodeStar. They should not be modified manually. If you want to add or change permissions, attach additional policies to the IAM user.

When you add a user to a project and choose a role for the user, the appropriate policy is applied automatically to the IAM user. Under most circumstances, you don't need to directly attach or manage policies or permissions in IAM. Manually attaching an AWS CodeStar role policy to an IAM user is not recommended. If absolutely necessary, as a supplement to an AWS CodeStar role policy, you can create your own managed policies to apply your own level of permissions to an IAM user.

Note
The policies for roles in an AWS CodeStar project apply to that project only. This helps ensure that users can only see and interact with the AWS CodeStar projects they have permissions to, at the level determined by their

role. Only users who will create AWS CodeStar projects should have a policy applied that allows access to all AWS CodeStar resources, regardless of project.

All AWS CodeStar role policies vary, depending on the AWS resources associated with the project with which the roles are associated. Unlike other AWS services, these policies are customized when the project is created and updated as project resources change. Therefore, there is no one canonical Owner, Contributor, or Viewer managed policy.

AWS CodeStar Owner Role Policy

The CodeStar_*project-id*_Owner managed policy allows a user to perform all actions in the AWS CodeStar project with no restrictions. This is the only policy that allows a user to add or remove team members. Although the contents of the policy vary, depending on the resources associated with the project, the CodeStar_*project-id*_Owner managed policy contains the following AWS CodeStar permissions. As an AWS managed policy, it is subject to change without notice.

```
1  ...
2  {
3    "Effect": "Allow",
4    "Action": [
5      ...
6      "codestar:*",
7      ...
8    ],
9    "Resource": [
10     "arn:aws:codestar:us-east-2:111111111111:project/project-id",
11     "arn:aws:iam::account-id:policy/CodeStar_project-id_Owner"
12    ]
13 },
14 {
15   "Effect": "Allow",
16   "Action": [
17     "codestar:DescribeUserProfile",
18     "codestar:ListProjects",
19     "codestar:ListUserProfiles",
20     "codestar:VerifyServiceRole",
21     ...
22   ],
23   "Resource": [
24     "*"
25   ]
26 },
27 {
28   "Effect": "Allow",
29   "Action": [
30     "codestar:*UserProfile",
31     ...
32   ],
33   "Resource": [
34     "arn:aws:iam::account-id:user/user-name"
35   ]
36 }
37 ...
```

An IAM user with this policy can perform all AWS CodeStar actions in the project, but unlike an IAM user

100

with the **AWSCodeStarFullAccess** policy, the user cannot create new projects. The `codestar:*` permission is limited in scope to a specific resource (the AWS CodeStar project associated with that project ID).

AWS CodeStar Contributor Role Policy

The CodeStar_*project-id*_Contributor managed policy allows a user to contribute to the project and change the project dashboard, but does not allow a user to add or remove team members. Although the contents of the policy vary, depending on the resources associated with the project, the CodeStar_*project-id*_Contributor policy contains the following AWS CodeStar permissions. As an AWS managed policy, it is subject to change without notice.

```
 1 ...
 2 {
 3   "Effect": "Allow",
 4   "Action": [
 5     ...
 6     "codestar:Describe*",
 7     "codestar:Get*",
 8     "codestar:List*",
 9     "codestar:PutExtendedAccess",
10     ...
11   ],
12   "Resource": [
13     "arn:aws:codestar:us-east-2:111111111111:project/project-id",
14     "arn:aws:iam::account-id:policy/CodeStar_project-id_Contributor"
15   ]
16 },
17 {
18   "Effect": "Allow",
19   "Action": [
20     "codestar:DescribeUserProfile",
21     "codestar:ListProjects",
22     "codestar:ListUserProfiles",
23     "codestar:VerifyServiceRole",
24     ...
25   ],
26   "Resource": [
27     "*"
28   ]
29 },
30 {
31   "Effect": "Allow",
32   "Action": [
33     "codestar:*UserProfile",
34     ...
35   ],
36   "Resource": [
37     "arn:aws:iam::account-id:user/user-name"
38   ]
39 }
40 ...
```

AWS CodeStar Viewer Role Policy

The CodeStar_*project-id*_Viewer managed policy allows a user to view a project in AWS CodeStar, but not change its resources or add or remove team members. Although the contents of the policy vary, depending on the resources associated with the project, the CodeStar_*project-id*_Viewer policy contains the following AWS CodeStar permissions. As an AWS managed policy, it is subject to change without notice.

```
 1  ...
 2  {
 3    "Effect": "Allow",
 4    "Action": [
 5      ...
 6      "codestar:Describe*",
 7      "codestar:Get*",
 8      "codestar:List*",
 9      ...
10    ],
11    "Resource": [
12      "arn:aws:codestar:us-east-2:111111111111:project/project-id",
13      "arn:aws:iam::account-id:policy/CodeStar_project-id_Viewer"
14    ]
15  },
16  {
17    "Effect": "Allow",
18    "Action": [
19      "codestar:DescribeUserProfile",
20      "codestar:ListProjects",
21      "codestar:ListUserProfiles",
22      "codestar:VerifyServiceRole",
23      ...
24    ],
25    "Resource": [
26      "*"
27    ]
28  },
29  {
30    "Effect": "Allow",
31    "Action": [
32      "codestar:*UserProfile",
33      ...
34    ],
35    "Resource": [
36      "arn:aws:iam::account-id:user/user-name"
37    ]
38  }
39  ...
```

IAM User Access to AWS CodeStar

When you add an IAM user to a project and choose a role for the user, AWS CodeStar applies the appropriate policy to the IAM user automatically. For IAM users, you don't need to directly attach or manage policies or permissions in IAM.

Add an IAM User to Your AWS CodeStar Project

After you create your AWS CodeStar project, grant IAM users access to your project. As an IAM user with the Owner role in an AWS CodeStar project or the **AWSCodeStarFullAccess** policy applied to your IAM user, you can add other IAM users to the project team. When you select the project-level role for the team member, AWS CodeStar attaches the appropriate managed policy to the IAM user based on the role you choose:

- Owner
- Contributor
- Viewer

Remove an IAM User from Your AWS CodeStar Project

When you delete a project, AWS CodeStar removes the policies that were applied automatically to IAM users that you added as team members. For IAM users, you don't need to directly detach or manage policies or permissions in IAM.

Attach an Inline Policy to an IAM User

When you add a user to a project, AWS CodeStar automatically attaches the managed policy for the project that matches the user's role. You should not manually attach an AWS CodeStar managed policy for a project to an IAM user. With the exception of AWSCodeStarFullAccess, we do not recommend that you attach policies that change an IAM user's permissions in an AWS CodeStar project. If you decide to create and attach your own policies, do the following:

1. Sign in to the AWS Management Console and open the IAM console at https://console.aws.amazon.com/iam/.

2. In the IAM console, in the navigation pane, choose **Users**, and then choose the user to which you want to attach additional policies.

3. On the **Permissions** tab, choose **Add permissions**. Choose **Attach existing policies directly**, select the policy you want to apply, and then choose **Attach Policy**.

   For example, if you want to add your own customized policy to a user, choose the policy name from the list of policies.

4. If you do not want to attach an existing policy but instead want to create your own custom policy, on the **Permissions** tab, choose **Add inline policy**. Choose **Custom Policy**, and then choose **Select**.

   In **Policy Name**, type a name for this policy. In the **Policy Document** box, type a policy that follows this format, and then choose **Apply Policy**:

```
1  {
2    "Version": "2012-10-17",
3    "Statement" : [
4      {
5        "Effect" : "Allow",
6        "Action" : [
7          "action-statement"
8        ],
9        "Resource" : [
10         "resource-statement"
11       ]
12     },
13     {
14       "Effect" : "Allow",
```

```
15      "Action" : [
16        "action-statement"
17      ],
18      "Resource" : [
19        "resource-statement"
20      ]
21    }
22  ]
23 }
```

In the preceding statement, for *action-statement* and *resource-statement*, specify the AWS CodeStar actions and resources the IAM user is allowed to perform or access. (By default, the IAM user does not have permissions unless a corresponding `Allow` statement is explicitly stated. If you want to specifically deny a permission granted by another policy, such as the policy for an AWS CodeStar role, choose `Deny` instead of Allow.) You can add statements as needed. The following sections describe the format of allowed actions and resources for AWS CodeStar. Syntax examples are provided in these sections.

Federated User Access to AWS CodeStar

Instead of creating an IAM user or using the root user, you can use user identities from AWS Directory Service, your enterprise user directory, a web identity provider, or IAM users assuming roles. These are known as *federated users*.

Grant federated users access to your AWS CodeStar project by manually attaching the managed policies described in AWS CodeStar Project-Level Policies and Permissions to the user's IAM role. You wait to attach the Owner, Contributor, or Viewer policy until after AWS CodeStar creates your project resources and IAM roles.

**Prerequisites: **

- You must have set up an identity provider. For more information, see Creating IAM Identity Providers. For example, have a SAML identity provider set up and AWS authentication set up through the provider. For more information about SAML federation, see About SAML 2.0-based Federation.
- You must have created a role for a federated user to assume when access is requested through an identity provider. An STS trust policy must be attached to the role that allows federated users to assume the role. For more information, see Federated Users and Roles in the *IAM User Guide*.
- You must have created your AWS CodeStar project and know the project ID.

For more information about creating a role for identity providers, see Creating a Role for a Third-Party Identity Provider (Federation).

Attach the `AWSCodeStarFullAccess` Managed Policy to the Federated User's Role

Grant a federated user permissions to create a project by attaching the `AWSCodeStarFullAccess` managed policy. To perform these steps, you must have signed in to the console either as a root user, an IAM administrator user in the account, or an IAM user or federated user with the associated AdministratorAccess managed policy or equivalent.

Note
After you create the project, your project Owner permissions are not applied automatically. Using a role with administrative permissions for your account, attach the Owner managed policy as detailed in Attach Your Project's AWS CodeStar Viewer/Contributor/Owner Managed Policy to the Federated User's Role.

1. Open the IAM console. In the navigation pane, choose **Policies**.

2. Enter `AWSCodeStarFullAccess` in the search field. The policy name is displayed, with a policy type of **AWS managed.** You can expand the policy to see the permissions in the policy statement.

3. Select the circle next to the policy, and then under **Policy actions**, choose **Attach**.

4. On the **Summary** page, choose the **Attached entities** tab. Choose **Attach**.

5. On the **Attach Policy** page, filter for the federated user's role in the search field. Select the box next to the name of the role and then choose **Attach policy**. The **Attached entities** tab shows the new attachment.

Attach Your Project's AWS CodeStar Viewer/Contributor/Owner Managed Policy to the Federated User's Role

Grant federated users access to your project by attaching the appropriate Owner, Contributor, or Viewer managed policy to the user's role. The managed policy gives the appropriate level of permissions. Unlike IAM users, you need to manually attach and detach managed policies for federated users. This is equivalent to assigning project permissions to team members in AWS CodeStar. To perform these steps, you must have signed in to the console either as a root user, an IAM administrator user in the account, or an IAM user or federated user with the associated AdministratorAccess managed policy or equivalent.

Prerequisities:

- You must have created a role or have an existing role that your federated user assumes.
- You must know which level of permissions you want to grant. The managed policies attached to the Owner, Contributor, and Viewer roles provide role-based permissions for your project.
- Your AWS CodeStar project must have been created. The managed policy is not available in IAM until the project is created.

1. Open the IAM console. In the navigation pane, choose **Policies**.

2. Enter your project ID in the search field. The policy name matching your project is displayed, with a policy type of **Customer managed**. You can expand the policy to see the permissions in the policy statement.

3. Choose one of these managed policies. This example attaches a Viewer managed policy. Select the circle next to the policy, and then under **Policy actions**, choose **Attach**.

4. On the **Summary** page, choose the **Attached entities** tab. Choose **Attach**.

5. On the **Attach Policy** page, filter for the federated user's role in the search field. Select the box next to the name of the role and then choose **Attach policy**. The **Attached entities** tab shows the new attachment.

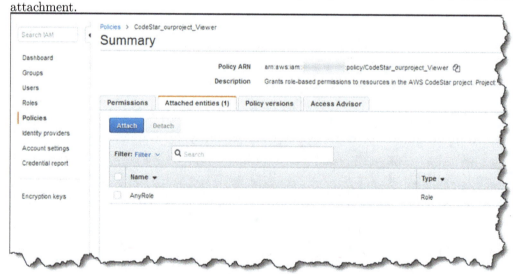

Detach an AWS CodeStar Managed Policy from the Federated User's Role

Before you delete your AWS CodeStar project, you must manually detach any managed policies you attached to a federated user's role. To perform these steps, you must have signed in to the console either as a root user, an IAM administrator user in the account, or an IAM user or federated user with the associated AdministratorAccess managed policy or equivalent.

1. Open the IAM console. In the navigation pane of the console, choose **Policies**.

2. Enter your project ID in the search field.

3. Select the circle next to the policy, and then under **Policy actions**, choose **Attach**.

4. On the **Summary** page, choose the **Attached entities** tab.

5. Filter for the federated user's role in the search field. Choose **Detach**.

Attach an AWS Cloud9 Managed Policy to the Federated User's Role

Grant federated users access to your AWS Cloud9 environment by attaching the `AWSCloud9User` managed policy to the user's role. Unlike IAM users, you must manually attach and detach managed policies for federated users. To perform these steps, you must have signed in to the console either as a root user, an IAM administrator user in the account, or an IAM user or federated user with the associated AdministratorAccess managed policy or equivalent.

Prerequisities:

- You must have created a role or have an existing role that your federated user assumes.
- You must know which level of permissions you want to grant:
  - The `AWSCloud9User` managed policy allows the user to do the following:
    - Create their own AWS Cloud9 development environments.
    - Get information about their own environments.
    - Change the settings for their own environments.
  - The `AWSCloud9Administrator` managed policy allows the user to do the following:
    - Create environments for themselves or others.
    - Get information about environments for themselves or others.
    - Delete environments for themselves or others.
    - Change the settings of environments for themselves or others.

1. Open the IAM console. In the navigation pane of the console, choose **Policies**.

2. Enter the policy name in the search field. This example searches for the `AWSCloud9User` managed policy. The managed policy is displayed, with a policy type of **AWS managed**. You can expand the policy to see the permissions in the policy statement.

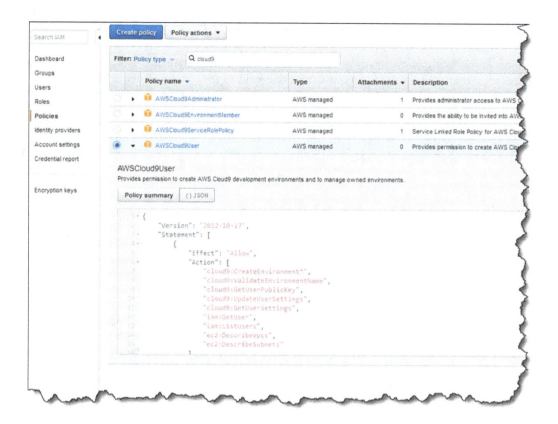

3. Choose one of these managed policies. This example attaches the `AWSCloud9User` managed policy. Select the circle next to the policy, and then under **Policy actions**, choose **Attach**.

4. On the **Summary** page, choose the **Attached entities** tab. Choose **Attach**.

5. On the **Attach Policy** page, filter for the federated user's role in the search field. Choose the box next to the name of the role and then choose **Attach policy**. The **Attached entities** tab shows the new attachment.

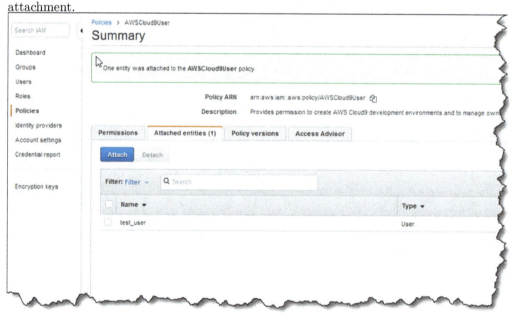

Detach an AWS Cloud9 Managed Policy from the Federated User's Role

To remove a federated user's AWS Cloud9 permissions, detach the policy. To perform these steps, you must have signed in to the console either as a root user, an IAM administrator user in the account, or an IAM user or federated user with the associated AdministratorAccess managed policy or equivalent.

1. Open the IAM console. In the navigation pane of the console, choose **Policies**.

2. Enter your project name in the search field.

3. Select the circle next to the policy and then under **Policy actions**, choose **Attach**.

4. On the **Summary** page, choose the **Attached entities** tab.

5. Filter for the federated user's role in the search field. Choose **Detach**.

AWS CodeStar Service Role Policy and Permissions

AWS CodeStar uses a service role, aws-codestar-service-role, when creating and managing the resources for your project. For more information, see "AWS service role" in Roles Terms and Concepts in the *IAM User Guide*.

Important
You must be signed in as an IAM administrator user or root account in order to create this service role. For more information, see First-Time Access Only: Your Root User Credentials and Creating Your First IAM Admin User and Group in the *IAM User Guide*.

This role is created for you the first time you create a project in AWS CodeStar. The service role acts on your behalf to create the resources you choose when creating a project and to display information about those resources in the AWS CodeStar project dashboard. It also acts on your behalf when you manage the resources for a project. It contains the following policy statement:

```
1  {
2    "Version": "2012-10-17",
3    "Statement": [
4      {
5        "Sid": "ProjectStack",
6        "Effect": "Allow",
7        "Action": [
8          "cloudformation:*Stack*",
9          "cloudformation:*ChangeSet*",
10         "cloudformation:GetTemplate"
11       ],
12       "Resource": [
13         "arn:aws:cloudformation:*:*:stack/awscodestar-*",
14         "arn:aws:cloudformation:*:*:stack/awseb-*",
15         "arn:aws:cloudformation:*:*:stack/aws-cloud9-*",
16         "arn:aws:cloudformation:*:aws:transform/CodeStar*"
17       ]
18     },
19     {
20       "Sid": "ProjectStackTemplate",
21       "Effect": "Allow",
22       "Action": [
23         "cloudformation:GetTemplateSummary",
24         "cloudformation:DescribeChangeSet"
25       ],
26       "Resource": "*"
27     },
```

```
28      {
29        "Sid": "ProjectQuickstarts",
30        "Effect": "Allow",
31        "Action": [
32          "s3:GetObject"
33        ],
34        "Resource": [
35          "arn:aws:s3:::awscodestar-*/*"
36        ]
37      },
38      {
39        "Sid": "ProjectS3Buckets",
40        "Effect": "Allow",
41        "Action": [
42          "s3:*"
43        ],
44        "Resource": [
45          "arn:aws:s3:::aws-codestar-*",
46          "arn:aws:s3:::aws-codestar-*/*",
47          "arn:aws:s3:::elasticbeanstalk-*",
48          "arn:aws:s3:::elasticbeanstalk-*/*"
49        ]
50      },
51      {
52        "Sid": "ProjectServices",
53        "Effect": "Allow",
54        "Action": [
55          "codestar:*Project",
56          "codestar:*Resource*",
57          "codestar:List*",
58          "codestar:Describe*",
59          "codestar:Get*",
60          "codestar:AssociateTeamMember",
61          "codecommit:*",
62          "codepipeline:*",
63          "codedeploy:*",
64          "codebuild:*",
65          "ec2:RunInstances",
66          "autoscaling:*",
67          "cloudwatch:Put*",
68          "ec2:*",
69          "elasticbeanstalk:*",
70          "elasticloadbalancing:*",
71          "iam:ListRoles",
72          "logs:*",
73          "sns:*",
74          "cloud9:CreateEnvironmentEC2",
75          "cloud9:DeleteEnvironmentEC2",
76          "cloud9:DescribeEnvironment*"
77        ],
78        "Resource": "*"
79      },
80      {
81        "Sid": "ProjectWorkerRoles",
```

```
82        "Effect": "Allow",
83        "Action": [
84          "iam:AttachRolePolicy",
85          "iam:CreateRole",
86          "iam:DeleteRole",
87          "iam:DeleteRolePolicy",
88          "iam:DetachRolePolicy",
89          "iam:GetRole",
90          "iam:PassRole",
91          "iam:PutRolePolicy",
92          "iam:SetDefaultPolicyVersion",
93          "iam:CreatePolicy",
94          "iam:DeletePolicy",
95          "iam:AddRoleToInstanceProfile",
96          "iam:CreateInstanceProfile",
97          "iam:DeleteInstanceProfile",
98          "iam:RemoveRoleFromInstanceProfile"
99        ],
100       "Resource": [
101         "arn:aws:iam::*:role/CodeStarWorker*",
102         "arn:aws:iam::*:policy/CodeStarWorker*",
103         "arn:aws:iam::*:instance-profile/awscodestar-*"
104       ]
105     },
106     {
107       "Sid": "ProjectTeamMembers",
108       "Effect": "Allow",
109       "Action": [
110         "iam:AttachUserPolicy",
111         "iam:DetachUserPolicy"
112       ],
113       "Resource": "*",
114       "Condition": {
115         "ArnEquals": {
116           "iam:PolicyArn": [
117             "arn:aws:iam::*:policy/CodeStar_*"
118           ]
119         }
120       }
121     },
122     {
123       "Sid": "ProjectRoles",
124       "Effect": "Allow",
125       "Action": [
126         "iam:CreatePolicy",
127         "iam:DeletePolicy",
128         "iam:CreatePolicyVersion",
129         "iam:DeletePolicyVersion",
130         "iam:ListEntitiesForPolicy",
131         "iam:ListPolicyVersions"
132       ],
133       "Resource": [
134         "arn:aws:iam::*:policy/CodeStar_*"
135       ]
```

```
136      },
137      {
138        "Sid": "InspectServiceRole",
139        "Effect": "Allow",
140        "Action": [
141          "iam:ListAttachedRolePolicies"
142        ],
143        "Resource": [
144          "arn:aws:iam::*:role/aws-codestar-service-role"
145        ]
146      },
147      {
148        "Sid": "IAMLinkRole",
149        "Effect": "Allow",
150        "Condition": {
151          "StringLike": {
152            "iam:AWSServiceName": "cloud9.amazonaws.com"
153          }
154        },
155        "Action": [
156          "iam:CreateServiceLinkedRole"
157        ],
158        "Resource": "arn:aws:iam::*:role/aws-service-role/cloud9.amazonaws.com/
                AWSServiceRoleForCloud9*"
159      }
160    ]
161 }
```

Action and Resource Syntax

The following sections describe the format for specifying actions and resources.

Actions follow this general format:

```
1 codestar:action
```

Where *action* is an available AWS CodeStar operation, such as `ListProjects` or `AssociateResource`. To allow an action, use the `"Effect" : "Allow"` clause. To explicitly deny an action, use the `"Effect" : "Deny"` clause. By default, all actions are denied, unless specified otherwise in any other attached policy.

Resources follow this general format:

```
1 arn:aws:codestar:region:account:resource-specifier
```

Where *region* is a target region (such as **us-east-2**), *account* is the AWS account ID, and *resource-specifier* is the project ID. Wildcard (*) characters can be used to specify a partial name.

For example, the following specifies the AWS CodeStar project named `my-first-projec` registered to the AWS account 111111111111 in the region **us-east-2**:

```
1 arn:aws:codestar:us-east-2:111111111111:project/my-first-projec
```

The following specifies any AWS CodeStar project that begins with the name `my-proj` registered to the AWS account 111111111111 in the region **us-east-2**:

```
1 arn:aws:codestar:us-east-2:111111111111:project/my-proj*
```

Topics

- Resource Scoping in AWS CodeStar
- Projects
- Resources
- Teams
- Users

Resource Scoping in AWS CodeStar

Some of the permissions in AWS CodeStar cannot be scoped to a resource, but instead must be scoped to all, or the action will fail.

The following action cannot be scoped. It must be set to *:

- ListProjects

Projects

Allowed actions include:

- `CreateProject` to create an AWS CodeStar project.
- `DeleteProject` to delete an AWS CodeStar project.
- `DescribeProject` to describe the attributes of an AWS CodeStar project.
- `ListProjects` to list all the AWS CodeStar projects.
- `UpdateProject` to update the attributes of an AWS CodeStar project.

The following example allows a specified IAM user to edit the attributes of an AWS CodeStar project, such as its project description:

```
1  {
2    "Version": "2012-10-17",
3    "Statement" : [
4      {
5        "Effect" : "Allow",
6        "Action" : [
7          "codestar:UpdateProject"
8        ],
9        "Resource" : "arn:aws:codestar:us-east-2:project/my-first-projec"
10     }
11   ]
12 }
```

Resources

Allowed actions include:

- `ListResources` to list all the resources for an AWS CodeStar project.

The following example allows an IAM user who has this policy attached to list resources for a project with the ID *my-first-projec*:

```
1  {
2    "Version": "2012-10-17",
3    "Statement" : [
4      {
5        "Effect" : "Allow",
```

```
6    "Action" : [
7      "codestar:ListResources",
8    ],
9    "Resource" : "arn:aws:codestar:us-east-2:project/my-first-projec"
10   }
11  ]
12 }
```

Teams

Allowed actions include:

- AssociateTeamMember to add a user to an AWS CodeStar project.
- DisassociateTeamMember to remove a user from an AWS CodeStar project.
- ListTeamMembers to list all the users in an AWS CodeStar project.
- UpdateTeamMember to change the team member's attributes in a AWS CodeStar project (for example, the user's project role).

The following example allows an IAM user who has this policy attached to add team members to an AWS CodeStar project with the project ID *my-first-projec*, but explicitly denies that user the ability to remove team members:

```
1  {
2    "Version": "2012-10-17",
3    "Statement" : [
4      {
5        "Effect" : "Allow",
6        "Action" : [
7          "codestar:AssociateTeamMember",
8        ],
9        "Resource" : "arn:aws:codestar:us-east-2:project/my-first-projec"
10     },
11     {
12       "Effect" : "Deny",
13       "Action" : [
14         "codestar:DisassociateTeamMember",
15       ],
16       "Resource" : "arn:aws:codestar:us-east-2:project/my-first-projec"
17     }
18    ]
19
20  ]
21 }
```

Users

Allowed actions include:

- CreateUserProfile to create a user profile in AWS CodeStar. This profile contains data associated with the user, such as a display name, that appears across all AWS CodeStar projects.
- DeleteUserProfile to delete an AWS CodeStar user profile.
- DescribeUserProfile to retrieve information about an AWS CodeStar user profile.
- ListUserProfiles to list all AWS CodeStar user profiles for an AWS account.
- UpdateUserProfile to update an AWS CodeStar profile for a user.

The following example allows an IAM user who has this policy attached to list all AWS CodeStar user profiles associated with an AWS account:

```
1  {
2    "Version": "2012-10-17",
3    "Statement" : [
4      {
5        "Effect" : "Allow",
6        "Action" : [
7          "codestar:ListUserProfiles",
8                  ],
9        "Resource" : "*"
10     }
11   ]
12 }
```

Logging AWS CodeStar API Calls with AWS CloudTrail

AWS CodeStar is integrated with CloudTrail, a service that captures API calls made by or on behalf of AWS CodeStar in your AWS account and delivers the log files to an Amazon S3 bucket you specify. CloudTrail captures API calls from the AWS CodeStar console, the AWS CLI, the AWS SDKs, and the AWS CodeStar HTTP API. Using the information collected by CloudTrail, you can determine which request was made to AWS CodeStar, the source IP address from which the request was made, who made the request, when it was made, and so on. To learn more about CloudTrail, including how to configure and enable it, see the AWS CloudTrail User Guide.

AWS CodeStar Information in CloudTrail

When CloudTrail logging is enabled in your AWS account, calls made to AWS CodeStar actions are tracked in log files. AWS CodeStar records are written together with other AWS service records in a log file. CloudTrail determines when to create and write to a new file based on a time period and file size.

All of the AWS CodeStar actions are logged. These actions are documented in the AWS CodeStar API Reference.

Every log entry contains information about who generated the request. The user identity information in the log helps you determine whether the request was made with root or IAM user credentials, with temporary security credentials for a role or federated user, or by another AWS service. For more information, see the `userIdentity` field in the CloudTrail Event Reference.

You can store your log files in your bucket for as long as you want, but you can also define Amazon S3 lifecycle rules to archive or delete log files automatically. By default, Amazon S3 server-side encryption (SSE) is used to encrypt your log files.

You can have CloudTrail publish Amazon SNS notifications when new log files are delivered. For more information, see Configuring Amazon SNS Notifications for CloudTrail.

You can also aggregate AWS CodeStar log files from multiple AWS regions and multiple AWS accounts into a single Amazon S3 bucket. For more information, see Receiving CloudTrail Log Files from Multiple Regions.

Understanding AWS CodeStar Log File Entries

CloudTrail log files can contain one or more log entries where each entry is made up of multiple JSON-formatted events. A log entry represents a single request from any source and includes information about the requested action, any parameters, the date and time of the action, and so on. The log entries are not guaranteed to be in any particular order. That is, they are not an ordered stack trace of the public calls.

The following example shows a CloudTrail log entry that demonstrates a `CreateProject` operation being called in AWS CodeStar:

```
1  {
2    "eventVersion": "1.05",
3    "userIdentity": {
4      "type": "AssumedRole",
5      "principalId": "AROAJLIN2OF3UBEXAMPLE:role-name",
6      "arn": "arn:aws:sts::account-ID:assumed-role/role-name/role-session-name",
7      "accountId": "account-ID",
8      "accessKeyId": "ASIAJ44LFQS5XEXAMPLE",
9      "sessionContext": {
10       "attributes": {
11         "mfaAuthenticated": "false",
12         "creationDate": "2017-06-04T23:56:57Z"
13       },
```

```
14        "sessionIssuer": {
15          "type": "Role",
16          "principalId": "AROAJLIN2OF3UBEXAMPLE",
17          "arn": "arn:aws:iam::account-ID:role/service-role/role-name",
18          "accountId": "account-ID",
19          "userName": "role-name"
20        }
21      },
22      "invokedBy": "codestar.amazonaws.com"
23    },
24    "eventTime": "2017-06-04T23:56:57Z",
25    "eventSource": "codestar.amazonaws.com",
26    "eventName": "CreateProject",
27    "awsRegion": "region-ID",
28    "sourceIPAddress": "codestar.amazonaws.com",
29    "userAgent": "codestar.amazonaws.com",
30    "requestParameters": {
31      "clientRequestToken": "arn:aws:cloudformation:region-ID:account-ID:stack/stack-name/
             additional-ID",
32      "id": "project-ID",
33      "stackId": "arn:aws:cloudformation:region-ID:account-ID:stack/stack-name/additional-ID",
34      "description": "AWS CodeStar created project",
35      "name": "project-name",
36      "projectTemplateId": "arn:aws:codestar:region-ID::project-template/project-template-name"
37    },
38    "responseElements": {
39      "projectTemplateId": "arn:aws:codestar:region-ID::project-template/project-template-name",
40      "arn": "arn:aws:codestar:us-east-1:account-ID:project/project-ID",
41      "clientRequestToken": "arn:aws:cloudformation:region-ID:account-ID:stack/stack-name/
             additional-ID",
42      "id": "project-ID"
43    },
44    "requestID": "7d7556d0-4981-11e7-a3bc-dd5daEXAMPLE",
45    "eventID": "6b0d6e28-7a1e-4a73-981b-c8fdbEXAMPLE",
46    "eventType": "AwsApiCall",
47    "recipientAccountId": "account-ID"
48 }
```

Limits in AWS CodeStar

The following table describes limits in AWS CodeStar. AWS CodeStar depends on other AWS services for project resources. Some of those service limits can be changed. For information about limits that can be changed, see AWS Service Limits.

Number of projects	Maximum of 333 projects in an AWS account. Actual limit will vary depending on the level of other service dependencies, for example the maximum number of pipelines in AWS CodePipeline allowed for your AWS account.
Number of AWS CodeStar projects to which an IAM user can belong	Maximum of 10 per individual IAM user.
Project IDs	Project IDs must be unique within an AWS account. Project IDs must be at least 2 characters and cannot exceed 15 characters. Allowed characters include: Letters a through z, inclusive. Numbers 0 through 9, inclusive. The special character - (minus sign). Any other characters, such as capital letters, spaces, . (period), @ (at sign), or _ (underscore), are not allowed.
Project names	Project names cannot exceed 100 characters in length, and cannot begin or end with an empty space.
Project descriptions	Any combination of characters between 0 and 1,024 characters in length. Project descriptions are optional.
Team members in an AWS CodeStar project	100
Display name in a user profile	Any combination of characters between 1 and 100 characters in length. Display names must include at least one character. That character cannot be a space. Display names cannot begin or end with a space.
Email address in a user profile	The email address must include an @ and end in a valid domain extension.
Federated access, root account access, or temporary access to AWS CodeStar	AWS CodeStar supports federated users and use of temporary access credentials. Using AWS CodeStar with a root account is not recommended.
IAM roles	A maximum of 5,120 characters in any managed policy that is attached to an IAM role.

Troubleshooting AWS CodeStar

The following information might help you troubleshoot common issues in AWS CodeStar.

Topics

- Project creation failure: A project was not created
- Project creation: I see an error when I try to edit Amazon EC2 configuration when creating a project
- Project deletion: An AWS CodeStar project was deleted, but resources still exist
- Team management failure: An IAM user could not be added to a team in an AWS CodeStar project
- Access failure: A federated user cannot access an AWS CodeStar project
- Access failure: A federated user cannot access or create an AWS Cloud9 environment
- Access failure: A federated user can create an AWS CodeStar project, but cannot view project resources
- Service role issue: The service role could not be created
- Service role issue: The service role is not valid or missing
- Project role issue: AWS Elastic Beanstalk health status checks fail for instances in an AWS CodeStar project
- Project role issue: A project role is not valid or missing
- Project extensions: Can't connect to JIRA
- GitHub: Can't access a repository's commit history, issues, or code

Project creation failure: A project was not created

Problem: When you try to create a project, you see a message that the creation failed.

Possible fixes: The most common reasons for failure are:

- A project with that ID already exists in your AWS account, possibly in a different region.
- The IAM user you used to sign in to the AWS Management Console does not have the permissions required to create a project.
- The AWS CodeStar service role is missing one or more required permissions.
- You have reached the maximum limit for one or more resources for a project (such as the limit on customer managed policies in IAM, Amazon S3 buckets, or pipelines in AWS CodePipeline).

Before you create a project, verify that you have the **AWSCodeStarFullAccess** policy applied to your IAM user. For more information, see AWS CodeStar Access Permissions Reference.

When you create a project, make sure that the ID is unique and meets the AWS CodeStar requirements. Be sure you selected the **AWS CodeStar would like permission to administer AWS resources on your behalf** check box.

To troubleshoot other issues, open the AWS CloudFormation console, choose the stack for the project you tried to create, and choose the **Events** tab. There might be more than one stack for a project. The stack names will start with `awscodestar-`, followed by the project ID. Stacks might be under the **Deleted** filter view. Review any failure messages in the stack events and correct the issue listed as the cause of those failures.

Project creation: I see an error when I try to edit Amazon EC2 configuration when creating a project

Problem: When you edit the Amazon EC2 configuration options during project creation, you see an error message or greyed-out option, and cannot continue with project creation.

Possible fixes: The most common reasons for an error message are:

- The VPC in the AWS CodeStar project template (either the default VPC, or the one used when the Amazon EC2 configuration was edited) has dedicated instance tenancy, and the instance type is not supported for dedicated instances. Either choose a different instance type or a different Amazon VPC.

- Your AWS account has no Amazon VPCs. You might have deleted the default VPC, and not created any others. Open the Amazon VPC console at https://console.aws.amazon.com/vpc/, choose **Your VPCs**, and make sure that you have at least one VPC configured. If not, create one. For more information, see Amazon Virtual Private Cloud Overview in the *Amazon VPC Getting Started Guide*.
- The Amazon VPC does not have any subnets. Choose a different VPC, or create a subnet for that VPC. For more information, see VPC and Subnet Basics.

Project deletion: An AWS CodeStar project was deleted, but resources still exist

Problem: An AWS CodeStar project was deleted, but resources created for that project still exist. By default, AWS CodeStar deletes project resources when the project is deleted. Some resources, such as Amazon S3 buckets, are retained even if the user selects the **Delete associated resources along with AWS CodeStar project** check box, as the buckets might contain data.

Possible fixes: Open the AWS CloudFormation console and find one or more of the AWS CloudFormation stacks used to create the project. The stack names will start with awscodestar-, followed by the project ID. The stacks might be under the **Deleted** filter view. Review the events associated with the stack to discover the resources created for the project. Open the console for each of those resources in the region where you created the AWS CodeStar project, and then manually delete the resources for that deleted project.

Project resources that might remain include:

- One or more project buckets in Amazon S3. Unlike other project resources, project buckets in Amazon S3 are not deleted when the **Delete associated AWS resources along with AWS CodeStar project** check box is selected.

  Open the Amazon S3 console at https://console.aws.amazon.com/s3/.

- A source repository for your project in AWS CodeCommit.

  Open the AWS CodeCommit console at https://console.aws.amazon.com/codecommit/.

- A pipeline for your project in AWS CodePipeline.

  Open the AWS CodePipeline console at https://console.aws.amazon.com/codepipeline/.

- An application and associated deployment groups in AWS CodeDeploy.

  Open the AWS CodeDeploy console at https://console.aws.amazon.com/codedeploy/.

- An application and associated environments in AWS Elastic Beanstalk.

  Open the Elastic Beanstalk console at https://console.aws.amazon.com/elasticbeanstalk/.

- A function in AWS Lambda.

  Open the AWS Lambda console at https://console.aws.amazon.com/lambda/.

- One or more APIs in API Gateway.

  Open the API Gateway console at https://console.aws.amazon.com/apigateway/.

- One or more IAM policies or roles in IAM.

  Sign in to the AWS Management Console and open the IAM console at https://console.aws.amazon.com/iam/.

- An instance in Amazon Elastic Compute Cloud (Amazon EC2).

  Open the Amazon EC2 console at https://console.aws.amazon.com/ec2/.

- One or more development environments in AWS Cloud9.

  To view, access, and manage development environments, open the AWS Cloud9 console at https://console.aws.amazon.com/cloud9/.

If your project uses resources outside of AWS, for example a GitHub repository or issues in Atlassian JIRA, those resources are not deleted, even if the **Delete associated AWS resources along with CodeStar project** box is selected.

Team management failure: An IAM user could not be added to a team in an AWS CodeStar project

Problem: When you try to add a user to a project, you see an error message saying that the addition failed.

Possible fixes: The most common reason for this error is that the IAM user has reached the limit of managed policies that can be applied to a user in IAM. You might also receive this error if you are not a member of the Owner role in the AWS CodeStar project where you tried to add the user, or if the IAM user does not exist or was deleted.

Make sure you are signed in as an IAM user who is an owner in that AWS CodeStar project. For more information, see Add Team Members to an AWS CodeStar Project .

To troubleshoot other issues, open the IAM console, choose the user you tried to add, and check how many managed policies are applied to that IAM user.

For more information, see Limitations on IAM Entities and Objects. For limits that can be changed, see AWS Service Limits.

Access failure: A federated user cannot access an AWS CodeStar project

Problem: A federated user is unable to see projects in the AWS CodeStar console.

Possible fixes: If you are signed in as a federated user, make sure you have the appropriate managed policy attached to the role you assume to sign in. For more information, see Attach Your Project's AWS CodeStar Viewer/Contributor/Owner Managed Policy to the Federated User's Role.

Add federated users to your AWS Cloud9 environment by manually attaching policies. See Attach an AWS Cloud9 Managed Policy to the Federated User's Role.

Access failure: A federated user cannot access or create an AWS Cloud9 environment

Problem: A federated user is unable to see or create an AWS Cloud9 environment in the AWS Cloud9 console.

Possible fixes: If you are signed in as a federated user, make sure you have the appropriate managed policy attached to the federated user's role.

You add federated users to your AWS Cloud9 environment by manually attaching policies to the federated user's role. See Attach an AWS Cloud9 Managed Policy to the Federated User's Role.

Access failure: A federated user can create an AWS CodeStar project, but cannot view project resources

Problem: A federated user was able to create a project, but cannot view project resources, such as the project pipeline.

Possible fixes: If you have attached the **AWSCodeStarFullAccess** managed policy, you have permissions to create a project in AWS CodeStar. However, to access all project resources, you must attach the Owner managed policy.

After AWS CodeStar creates the project resources, project permissions to all project resources are available in the Owner, Contributer, and Viewer managed policies. You must manually attach the Owner policy to your role to access all of the resources. See Configure Permissions for Federated Users.

Service role issue: The service role could not be created

Problem: When you try to create a project in AWS CodeStar, you see a message prompting you to create the service role. When you choose the option to create it, you see an error.

Possible fixes: The most common reason for this error is that you are logged into AWS with an account that does not have sufficient permissions to create the service role. To create the AWS CodeStar service role (`aws-codestar-service-role`), you must be logged in as an administrative user or with a root account. Log out of the console, and log back in with an IAM user that has the `AdministratorAccess` managed policy applied.

Service role issue: The service role is not valid or missing

Problem: When you open the AWS CodeStar console, you see a message indicating the AWS CodeStar service role is missing or not valid.

Possible fixes: The most common reason for this error is that an administrative user edited or deleted the service role (`aws-codestar-service-role`). If the service role was deleted, you will be prompted to create it. You must be logged in as an administrative user or with a root account to create the role. If the role was edited, it is no longer valid. Log in to the IAM console as an administrative user, find the service role in the list of roles, and delete it. Switch to the AWS CodeStar console and follow the on-screen instructions to create the service role.

Project role issue: AWS Elastic Beanstalk health status checks fail for instances in an AWS CodeStar project

Problem: If you created an AWS CodeStar project that includes Elastic Beanstalk before September 22, 2017, Elastic Beanstalk health status checks might fail. If you have not changed the Elastic Beanstalk configuration since you created the project, the health status check fails and reports a grey state. Despite the health check failure, your application should still run as expected. If you changed the Elastic Beanstalk configuration since you created the project, the health status check fails, and your application might not run correctly.

Fix: One or more IAM roles are missing required IAM policy statements. Add the missing policies to the affected roles in your AWS account.

1. Sign in to the AWS Management Console and open the IAM console at https://console.aws.amazon.com/iam/.

   (If you cannot do this, see your AWS account administrator for assistance.)

2. In the navigation pane, choose **Roles**.

3. In the list of roles, choose **CodeStarWorker-*Project-ID*-EB**, where *Project-ID* is the ID of one of the affected projects. (If you cannot easily find a role in the list, type some or all of the role's name in the **Search** box.)

4. On the **Permissions** tab, choose **Attach Policy**.

5. In the list of policies, select **AWSElasticBeanstalkEnhancedHealth** and **AWSElasticBeanstalk-Service**. (If you cannot easily find a policy in the list, type some or all of the policy's name in the search box.)

6. Choose **Attach Policy**.

7. Repeat steps 3 through 6 for each affected role that has a name following the pattern **CodeStarWorker-** *Project-ID*-**EB**.

Project role issue: A project role is not valid or missing

Problem: When you try to add a user to a project, you see an error message saying that the addition failed because the policy for a project role is either missing or not valid.

Possible fixes: The most common reason for this error is that one or more project policies was edited in or deleted from IAM. Project policies are unique to AWS CodeStar projects, and cannot be recreated. The project cannot be used. Create a new project in AWS CodeStar, and migrate data to the new project. Clone project code from the unusable project's repository, and push that code to the new project's repository. Copy team wiki information from the old project to the new project. Add users to the new project. When you are sure you have migrated all data and settings, delete the unusable project.

Project extensions: Can't connect to JIRA

Problem: When you use the **Atlassian JIRA** extension to try to connect an AWS CodeStar project to a JIRA instance, the following message displays: "The URL is not a valid JIRA URL. Verify that the URL is correct."

Possible fixes:

- Make sure the JIRA URL is correct, and then try connecting again.
- Your self-hosted JIRA instance may not be accessible from the public Internet. Contact your network administrator to make sure your JIRA instance can be accessed from the public Internet, and then try connecting again.

GitHub: Can't access a repository's commit history, issues, or code

Problem: In the dashboard for a project that stores its code in GitHub, the **Commit history** and **GitHub Issues** tiles display a connection error, or choosing **Open in GitHub** or **Create issue** in these tiles displays an error.

Possible causes:

- The AWS CodeStar project may no longer have access to the GitHub repository.
- The repository may have been deleted or renamed in GitHub.

AWS CodeStar User Guide Release Notes

The following is summary information about significant updates to the *AWS CodeStar User Guide*.

Contents

- February 22, 2018
- February 14, 2018
- December 20, 2017
- November 30, 2017
- October 12, 2017
- August 17, 2017
- July 25, 2017
- June 14, 2017
- April 19, 2017

February 22, 2018

This guide is now available on GitHub. You can also use GitHub to submit feedback and change requests for this guide's content. For more information, choose the **Edit on GitHub** icon in the guide's navigation bar, or see the awsdocs/aws-codestar-user-guide repository on the GitHub website.

February 14, 2018

AWS CodeStar is now available in the Asia Pacific (Seoul) region. For more information, see AWS CodeStar in the *Amazon Web Services General Reference*.

December 20, 2017

AWS CodeStar is now available in the Asia Pacific (Tokyo) and Canada (Central) regions. For more information, see AWS CodeStar in the *Amazon Web Services General Reference*.

November 30, 2017

AWS CodeStar now supports using AWS Cloud9, a web browser-based online IDE, to work with project code. For more information, see Use AWS Cloud9 with AWS CodeStar.

For a list of supported AWS regions, see AWS Cloud9 in the *Amazon Web Services General Reference.*

October 12, 2017

AWS CodeStar now supports storing project code in GitHub. For more information, see Create a Project.

August 17, 2017

AWS CodeStar is now available in the US West (N. California) and EU (London) regions. For more information, see AWS CodeStar in the *Amazon Web Services General Reference*.

July 25, 2017

AWS CodeStar is now available in the Asia Pacific (Sydney), Asia Pacific (Singapore), and EU (Frankfurt) regions. For more information, see AWS CodeStar in the *Amazon Web Services General Reference.*

June 14, 2017

AWS CodeStar is now integrated with CloudTrail, a service that captures API calls made by or on behalf of AWS CodeStar in your AWS account and delivers the log files to an Amazon S3 bucket you specify. For more information, see Logging API Calls with CloudTrail.

April 19, 2017

This is the first release of the *AWS CodeStar User Guide.*

AWS Glossary

For the latest AWS terminology, see the AWS Glossary in the *AWS General Reference*.